Life Lessons from My Father

Life Lessons from My Father

Things Dad Used to Say

John Fouts Gardenhire

B
GAR
GAR

To order additional copies of this book, contact:
Xlibris Corporation
1-888-795-4274
www.Xlibris.com
Orders@Xlibris.com
28718

Contents

ACKNOWLEDGMENTS

I offer my grateful thanks to my wife, Lucy Kinchen, for giving me the title of this book and for her many corrections and editorial suggestions throughout the writing of this text. And to my daughter, Alissa Dawn Gardenhire-Crooks, many thanks as well, for without her queries about her grandfather and her suggestion that I compile his "sayings," this work would not exist.

AUTHOR'S NOTE

Two characters herein have fictitious names; otherwise, the whole of these illustrations is true. Also, some of the entries are the results of specific conversations with Alissa; therefore, I have included my answers in a structure much like how I'd responded to her during those talks.

INTRODUCTION TO DAD, SHIRLEY RICHARD GARDENHIRE

Shirley Richard Gardenhire was the most marvelous man whom I want to tell you about. Born in 1891 in the tiny town of Alma, Kansas, he grew up in this tiny German community where his was the only black family in town. His mother's illness forced the family to bring in a wet nurse from the community who lived with the Gardenhires for the first two and a half months of his life. This German lady continued to nurse Dad for eight months, making frequent road crossings to feed Dad. She would not accept any compensation for her services because she saw what she was doing as her duty to help out a neighbor who was in need. My Fouts cousins contended that that was where Dad got his blue eyes.

Making his way through the local schools there in Alma with a rather distinguished academic record, he matriculated at Kansas State College on a Latin scholarship, having been the top Latin scholar of his Alma High School's graduating class of 1911. This was remarkable in itself because there were not many black students going to college during that time, and there were even fewer who were going to college to study Latin.

When he graduated from Kansas State, Dad found very few employment opportunities open to him; so he, along with many other black men, [1] took a job at the Santa Fe Railroad Company as a "truck mechanic."[2]

---

[1]   Black men were treated badly by the railroad companies for a long time. These men who came into a difficult situation and quickly became master artisans in various skill areas were systematically denied promotions. Initially, the railroad companies tried to deprive these employees of any benefits. Again, the courts intervened and prevented the railroad companies from cutting off the health care coverage for these men and their family members. The railroad companies, however, managed to limit the medical coverage to the men only. The railroad companies, it was discovered many years later, also had a specific policy of not promoting black workers. It did not matter how skilled these men became or how loyal and efficient they became in their work. I know this for a fact because Dad invented several labor-saving tools that the Santa Fe "wrote up" in their manuals, but Dad got no credit for his ingenuity and imagination in that workplace.

[2]   "Truck" mechanics maintained the wheels of a railroad car.

11

During the strike, Dad did his part by being a strike breaker. When the strike ended, the railroad companies, including the Santa Fe Railroad Company, tried to fire all of the newly hired black employees. The courts enjoined every one of the railroad companies from firing these newly hired men. Since this job with the Santa Fe Railroad Company was considered to be a "very good job" with pay that was not available to black men of that period, he, like many other black men, remained with the railroad for all of his working life. This job permitted him to support himself, his wife, and their children in a very middle-class lifestyle with confidence and dignity. And that is where I come into this story. This man, Shirley Richard Gardenhire, was my father.

Of all the wonderful qualities that I could share about Dad, it is his parenting skill that I want to present in this book. Dad parented the three of us—Shirley Richard Gardenhire Jr., Ruth Ann Gardenhire-Johnson, and me, John Fouts Gardenhire—wisely and thoughtfully using sayings as a very accessible instructional tool. He had a myriad of them, many of which I shall share with you in this book. It was through these many sayings that he showed us ways to solve problems of growing up as well as ways to develop and maintain both our self-respect and respect for others.

The evidence of the force and power of his chosen parenting technique is revealed through the lives of the three of us. The lives of my two siblings and my own clearly prove that his theory and plan of raising his children worked well. All of us are responsible and successful citizens: Richard is a retired "supercargo" longshoreman; Ruth, a dietitian and owner of an architectural engineering firm; and me, a retired college professor. And in a direct line from Dad through me is my beloved daughter, Alissa Dawn Gardenhire-Crooks, PhD and a gainfully employed MDRC research associate and coauthor of this book.

The last time I talked with Dad, he told me he was glad that he was able to live to see the result of his handiwork as represented by the success of each one of us. His satisfaction with us was written all over his face, and then he said to me, "I have done all that a man gets to do in his life. I fell in love and lived to see my children happy— you are happy, aren't you? he laughed—independent, successful people. That's all you get! There isn't any more. I am very content." After a thought-filled pause, he added, "When you ask more from life than life has to offer, you will always be disappointed. The same is true of marriage. Don't ask more from it than it can offer. Choose carefully and go with what you have chosen."

So herein we shall present an important part of his story: the sayings that worked so well for me and my siblings.

1.   It does not hurt you to be nice to people.
2.   Treat yourself well.
3.   Always have more money than months.
4.   You are not better than anybody, but you are just as good as anybody.

5. You cannot spoil your children with affection.
6. Keep your friends by corresponding with them.
7. Study Latin.
8. You can always come home.
9. When you have lots to do, get off your bottom and go to work.
10. He who does not enjoy his own company can't be a good company.
11. Be at your best every day because you never know who is learning from you.
12. Refuse to live your life on other people's terms.
13. Walk in like you own the place.
14. Sex!
15. For you to be successful, you have to work harder, so do it.
16. Keep your money in things like real estate or gold.
17. Don't lend more than you can afford to give away.
18. Plan your work and work your plan.
19. Be on time.
20. Keep your business at home.
21. From observation, develop a play ritual with your partner.
22. Read the newspaper.
23. Never step on an ant that is not bothering you.
24. Discipline your children.
25. What they think does not change the color of ink.
26. Be satisfied only with the best work that you can do.
27. Always begin your essays with an adverb.
28. When shopping, always buy the best.
29. Compliment a bully.
30. Money is your freedom.
31. Hardly anything is ever all your fault.
32. Never get upset over nothing.
33. Always clean up your own messes.
34. Always take care of your pets.
35. Don't look for trouble. It can find you without your help.
36. Always put the lid on paint cans while you are painting.
37. Private thoughts should be just that.
38. Do what you want to do without hurting other people.
39. When criticized, look for the truth in it.
40. You hear best when you listen to what is being said to you.
41. Never argue with a fool in public. Guess why.
42. Don't overeat.

Dad held strong feelings about what he wanted for his kids, as I have said to you many times before. So to achieve his goals in parenting, as he conceived of that responsibility, Dad discussed ideas with us, as well as with each of us, from early on.

Ruth and Richard have corroborated this. I've checked with them on it. They agree that Dad talked about those ideas around us and with each of us so that we would not miss or misunderstand those concepts and feelings of his. He would mix these "idea discussions injection" with his conversation at almost any time and with almost anyone, often as an aside to one of us. Should I be listening to the adults discussing whatever topic of the day, Dad would be sure to include one of his "ideas" to be sure that I got it. Often, he would do this with a smile or a chuckle once he was sure that I heard and understood it.

Dad loved to reinforce his points to us with illustrations about people who have done well. I can just hear him saying in his discussions with whomever, "Look, traditionally, effective, successful people are viewed as perfect; that is, their lives are assumed to be without difficulties or problems or challenges of any kind. The fact is that these kinds of people function well in spite of the difficulties and challenges that they face." Dad really believed in "success models" and often cited examples of people who had "overcome." He might have used a multisyllabic verb to make his argument more profound, not to mention grander.

"Successful people are not dismayed by their problems or defeated by them. Rather, they choose to pursue their goals and achieve great things while managing their personal challenges so that the rest of us do not notice. And that is as it should be. Their problems are none of our business. We don't want to know about them. We want to know about their accomplishments. The things that they do often without assistance or applause are all that we want to know about." So you see, Dad wanted to have examples in front of us of ideas about how to become successful. And that is why he worked so hard to produce what he hoped for—effective, successful, responsible adult citizens.

I believe that he succeeded in that endeavor by teaching life lessons via his life example and via his sharing of his many life-affirming sayings, a list of which is presented in this book.

Thoughtful and successful child rearing had been presenting a paramount challenge to parents in any age from the time of the *Homo erectus* onward. The stereotype of male parents in our most recent decades presents a man who is somewhat detached from the grindingly difficult ongoing minutia of daily parenting. This might be true for some men, but for my father, this stereotype was far from the truth. By contrast to the unseeing stereotype, my father, Shirley Richard Gardenhire, participated in our rearing mightily; and he did so with warmth, affection, alertness, style, firmness, and good humor.

Looking back on how my father engaged us when we were growing up, I can discern a clear strategy of parenting that he employed. The first was to be available to and for us whenever he was home. And the second strategy was to talk to us, covering the widest range of topics. No subject was off-limits at 807 Wood Street. Dad and Mother encouraged us to talk to them about what was interesting to us at the moment. He said that we could bring any topic home, and from his behavior, he meant just that. Even when I came home from junior high school one afternoon and over dinner offered that Hearldean said that Ms. Mary was a prostitute. During the very brief shocked silence that followed my bombshell, I was also able to ask the next question, which was "What is a prostitute?" Well, Mother gave a textbook answer, finishing it up with the comment that I should stay away from Ms. Mary. Dinner at the Gardenhires was quite often interesting, if not downright exciting. So you see, that kind of conversation was encouraged at home for all of us!

One of the ways that he achieved his extraordinary involvement in our day-to-day parenting while working very long hours at two difficult, dangerous, and dirty jobs was via the good *words*, which he always gave to us as we—Shirley Richard Jr., Ruth Ann, and I, John Fouts—grew up in Topeka's Mud Town.

These good words took the form of sayings that he readily had at his command and which, as Mother used to say, "just rolled off his tongue." He was just full of aphorisms and sayings, which he made up as needed on the issue-driven spot. The effect it had on us was that we grew up with a wealth of behavioral controls that worked to keep us out of trouble and headed for responsible adult lives.

Dad cited the fact that when one talks with successful people, they will often tell you that their effectiveness results from the conscience's decision to "do well." Choices in their lives are not left to chance; that careful choice making was what he wanted for us. Dad understood that those kinds of choices were made out of life planning, which is required to obtain goals that need to be set early in the inchoate planners' lives. Much can be learned from the lessons that successful, effective people demonstrate in their lives daily, Dad believed; and he said so from time to time.

Adopting the ideas that we get from their examples, he often told us, offered to us a shortcut to successful lives. Dad believed that anyone could apply these models of successful people to one's own life, and by so doing, we could develop more self-esteeming new attitudes and organize our lives so that each of us could understand that everything that you can imagine is indeed possible.

With that foremost in our minds as we thought about, planned, and began to write this book, we chose a format that we hope will be immediately accessible and at once useful to each and every reader of this book. So that you will discover the wonderful qualities inside each one of you as you apply some of Dad's sayings to your daily lives.

The format that we are using here presents anecdotes that illustrate the point or points that each of Dad's sayings make. Our sincerest hope is that you enjoy Dad's ideas and benefit from reading them.

IT DOES NOT HURT YOU TO BE NICE TO PEOPLE

Dad used to say "It does not hurt you to be nice to people" a lot. One memorable illustration of this idea occurred while Ruth and I were awaiting the arrival of Richard. I was persuaded to take a guided bus tour of Chicago.[1] I did not want to go on the said tour, but to accommodate Ruth's wishes, I agreed to go with her. We found ourselves seated on the top deck of our tour bus, and two rows in front of us sat three Japanese gentlemen to whom nobody spoke. So in my best Japanese, I greeted them. They did not know that in doing so I had used the whole of my Japanese vocabulary. They were delighted that someone had tried to communicate with them and were effusive in their response. They proceeded to converse with us for the remainder of our tour. And upon our return to the bus terminal, they asked if I would like to come to Japan. Of course, I said that I would love to but that I had no plans to do so in the immediate future. Then I told them that should they ever come to San Francisco, they should call me, and I would be glad to give them a tour of the Bay Area. Our conversation ended with my invitation to them.

Thinking no more about it, I returned home. Well, not long after I got back home, our tour partners did indeed call; and I gave them—all four of them—the very best tour of the Bay Area that one long afternoon could provide. The two gentlemen had failed to mention that they had their wives with them when we met back in Chicago. I enjoyed that tour as much as they did. As we parted this time, the gentlemen repeated their question as to whether I would like to come to Japan, to which I answered in the affirmative again.

The next spring, I received a letter containing a first-class United Airlines ticket and an itinerary of speaking engagements at four Kensu training centers and at two women's universities as well. The engagement was to cover two months!

---

[1]   My sister, brother, and I have been spending a week together every year for over twenty years now. This week spent together found us in spots and places all over the world, from Marrakech to Tokyo and a lot of spots in between. During this particular year, the chosen travel spot was Chicago.

Needless to say, I went and had a wonderful time and made new friends as well. Of course, I was paid for my talks too. Another tour followed two years later, which was as marvelous as the first one.

So you see, it does not hurt to be nice to people! One *kanishiwa* goes a long way.

Dad practiced this saying. He made a point of being a resource for folks in the neighborhood. Sometimes this behavior provided a slight annoyance for Mother. Dad would say to her, "Old lady, it did not hurt me to lend a hand." She was persuaded and never carped about it beyond a single comment that I can remember. Dad also was nice to hobos. In those days, we did not have homeless people, save for hobos. They came to our door from time to time; and Dad saw to it that each one was fed and oftentimes given some waxed-paper-wrapped food or a piece of clothing, at least, to take with him. Mother was less generous in this matter, but she fed them too even when Dad was not at home when they knocked at our back door. Mother laughingly said that hobos had a mark on our house because so many came our way.

WALK IN LIKE YOU
OWN THE PLACE

Alissa, one of the things that I wish is that Dad had lived long enough to have been a nurturing part of your growing up. Your lives overlapped by only four months. We had tickets for Seattle when he died. We exchanged them for Topeka tickets so that we could bury him. At his wake, several people commented about this way* he had of "walking in like he owned the place." And the amazing thing was that they admired him for his style. His courage in the face of mildly segregated Topeka in the thirties, forties, fifties, and sixties gave strength to a number of these men who knew, respected, and valued your granddad. So these friends knew this phrase, and family members knew it well too because we heard it often, and we witnessed it being demonstrated by Dad many times.

I remember one time in particular where a lesser person might have been intimidated by the circumstances, in this instance, his going into the best men's store in Topeka to look at hats or, rather, a certain hat. All of the black folks in town knew very well that the best stores did not allow blacks to try on anything. And it was well-known that Ray Beers was the worst in this regard. Well, what they did not know was that Dad had his eye on a new Stetson hat called the Open Road and that he was intent on treating himself to one. The story goes (told by Mr. Irving, who worked there and observed the whole thing) that Dad walked into the shop, looked at a number of hats, which he proceeded to try on in front of the large mirror in the center of the shop. The sales personnel were so flustered by Dad's audacity when Dad grabbed his prized hat and announced that he would take it, plopping a one-hundred-dollar bill down on the counter as he spoke. The salesperson was so discombobulated that he meekly wrote up Dad's purchase and handed the nicely boxed and bagged purchase to Dad. Dad and his money talked! Dad walked out just as he had walked in.

I have had many of my own happy experiences with the walk-in-like-you-own-the-place attitude on display. Marsha Jane Fox Davis,[1] my friend of more than fifteen

---

[1] I took Marsha Jane Fox Davis, the aforementioned friend, to lunch in La Jolla. As we lunched at La Valencia's Sky Room Restaurant (today, rooms there range from $800 to $4,000 per day. It was, and still is, the place to stay when visiting in La Jolla) overlooking the beautiful Pacific,

years, told me recently that it was that attitude of mine that made her like me so much in the beginning of our friendship—in kindergarten!

And as I raised you, I taught and demonstrated the self-esteem-boosting reward of living without culture-assigned fears and limitations, which are all too readily dumped upon girls in general and upon blacks in particular—be they black male or black female!

I have always wanted you to fully understand and appreciate your granddad's saying because it is, when fully comprehended and appreciated, the oil on the hinges of the doors to comfortable assertiveness. Note the word "comfortable" here. For females, assertiveness is too often viewed as loud, pushy, unladylike, boorish, and even mean, while none of these adjectives would ever be used to characterize an assertive male. Knowing this about the "real world," I insisted that you have the awareness and insight needed to thrive assertively in that world. That is the reason why you heard it and a myriad of other mantras as you were growing up. I knew that your internalizing Dad's sayings would give you good working tools for functioning skillfully, and not to mention happily, in your adult life. When you think of the power that the words of the saying unleash within yourself, are you awed? I am. Think about it—own, own! You know that when you own something, ownership gives you dominion over it; owning something gives you space, a safe zone; owning

---

I was reminded of my first lunch in that spectacular room. I was eight or nine years old at the time and had often heard how lovely the La Valencia Hotel was from Uncle Jay and all of my aunts down there in La Jolla. I also knew that "we" were not welcome there. In those days, I walked all over La Jolla while they worked. The only restriction that they placed upon my movements was that I should not walk up to any of the homes where they were employed. This left me with lots of free time and free money too. When I arrived at 7415 Draper Avenue for the summer, Aunt Anna would always greet me with a $50 bill, saying that I should take it because she had been trying to get rid of it. So there I was with money in my pocket and all of the Village spread invitingly before of me. On one of those classic, lovely, temperate La Jolla summer days, I walked into La Valencia and announced that I wanted a hamburger. I remember that my arrival there caused a stir among the waiters and greeter, but presently, I was seated at a "single" table by the kitchen door but with a view of the ocean. (There is not a bad table in the room.) I ate my lunch. That lunch cost me $1.55. When I got home and began to tell them what I had done that day, all of the folks were startled. Neighbors and friends were called in to hear me tell of my escapade. They all repeated the "You can't go in there" admonitions. "John's going to get us all fired!" they shouted. Finally, Aunt Maude asked me how I had done it. I said that I had not thought about it at all and that "I just walked in like I owned the place." They all howled with laughter and repeated my story for many, many years.

I repeated the story to the present-day waiters as Marsha Jane and I left, and they got a big kick out of it too.

something gives you freedom to choose and behave as you like on your own timetable, on your own terms; owning something is comforting, blood-pressure lowering, and lots of other good stuff that you can think of once you begin to implement this attitude as you go about your daily business.

When you really learn this stuff, other additional life-affirming givens (that is, the way you are without having to think about it) will appear in your life. One main given is exhilaration in facing the world without fear of change. After all, one way for you to know that you are alive is when things change and you adapt with those changes. I know that you will be open to any new experiences. (Of course, when you are applying these ideas, you will already be at the make-good-choices level of "grownness.") Raising you, I planned to see you develop so that you were buoyed by the awareness of the fact that "you are equal to life's challenges" and the knowledge that you can handle any situation that arises because you are grounded in the assurances that without assistance or applause, you can accomplish whatever it is that you are to achieve in this moment. You see that the challenge before you is "doable" because you own it and not vice versa.

Since the messages that culture sends to girls is the exact opposite of the message that I knew you needed, I worked hard to show you another way. Although I am sure that you did not "get it" at first, I saw you employing this idea, and others too, so that I am reassured that you appreciate the wonder, majesty, and power of it very well indeed.

SAVE YOUR MONEY

Oh, when Dad said, "Save your money," it had real meaning for me early on in my growing up. The paramount importance of it was demonstrated to me when a man came to our door. I might have been ten years old at that time so that I was an observer of this event rather than a participant. This man was dressed in a suit and drove a big limousine—a green Packard automobile. He spoke in a booming voice that was out of proportion with the demands of the scene on our front porch at our front door with everybody within arm's length of one another.

The man demanded to see "Gardenhire," not "Mr. Gardenhire" or "your father"—just "Gardenhire" in this loud tone. This happened during the noon hour because Dad was at home and was expecting this "gentleman" to appear at our door on this particular date. You see, it was the date that the balloon payment on our house was due. The man announced this to Dad when he opened the screen door, adding, "I know you don't have the money for the payment, so I am here to take your house."

Everybody was invited into our house as courtesy. No such courtesy was extended to this boorish man. Instead, Dad came out on the front porch and spoke to him out there, saying, "If you just wait for a moment." Dad got his jacket and his Topeka First Federal Band book and told the man that he could follow Dad uptown to the bank where he would withdraw the funds to pay all of the balloon payment.

The man was stunned. He stuttered, backtracking, and said that they could refinance the loan and everything would be just as it was before. Dad assured him that would not be necessary, and all that he had to do was follow Dad to the bank to get the money for the loan payment. The man had no idea that not only did Dad understand what a balloon payment was when he signed the documents to buy 807 but he had also made arrangements for paying off that loan, balloon payment and all, on that very demand date. Dad had saved the money to "save our home" by working a second job for five years. Dad saved almost all of the money that he earned from that second job at Morrell's Meat Packing Company. As I remember, the balloon payment was only $4,000, which was quite a lot of money in those days.

I watched them drive off in tandem, Dad in his powder blue Cadillac and the man bringing up the dusty rear.

Dad told us how the first banker was shocked to find that at the Topeka First Federal Bank, Dad was known to the president of the bank, who greeted Dad warmly.

Unbeknownst to the man, Dad and the president of the TFFB were high school classmates and football-playing buddies who had stayed in touch with each other over the years, attending Kansas State College's football games together from time to time. They also attended several "army/navy" football games back east. The tickets for these games Dad obtained from one of his pen pals, one Dr. Jordan, a veterinarian and "navy man" who lived in Washington DC.

At the time Dad bought 807, he and his banker friend had discussed a way for Dad to make this payment by opening a savings account, which Dad did.

When Dad returned home from this episode, he took me aside and told me to be sure to "save your money" because you never know when you are going to need some, and sometimes you do know, and it is good to have it when those times arise.

All of this was said to me with a laugh and a hug. After this little talk, he jumped in our car and drove back to the shops.

ALWAYS HAVE MORE MONEY
THAN MONTHS

I must tell you about this saying that Dad offered up to us on every payday. On 807 Wood Street, his payday was everybody's payday, us kids' too. [1] Richard, Ruth, and I all had been getting an allowance from early on in our youth. Our allowance increased with our age, and he had this policy that increased our allowance by the amount that was left over from the past month's allowance so that he would give us the allowance plus the amount of money that we had returned unspent. Well, I soon learned to budget so that I always had some part of my allowance to show him at the end of every month. As a result of my early-learned budget management skills, I was sometimes doubling my allowance. Amused by my newly found thrift and by the accumulation of my cash funds, Dad would say that when I get rich, I should "keep your money in things like real estate and gold, things that you can touch." I got this same advice from a very wealthy friend of mine. He was a world-famous coin dealer who did as he told me to do.

By the way, much of the fun in saving my allowance lay in the fact that your aunt Ruth could never come to the end of the month with any money to show and always needed to borrow from me to make it. She never got it right! Yet Dad gave her extra money from time to time because "girls need more than boys."

While funding her, he would always admonish her that she needed to do better. "Get into the habit of saving some of your money every month," he would implore.

The value of the ideas and ideals represented in the sayings of Dad was wonderfully invaluable, and it continues to be that way for me. Many life-affirming lessons have been taught with these sayings, chief among which was the idea that managing your economic life carefully made your life easier because "money is your

---

[1] Payday at 807 saw Dad coming home and presenting his freshly cashed check funds to Mother, our bookkeeping financial manager at 807. Each and every time that he did so, she asked him, "How much do you want, Sherl?" That was the only time that she used a nickname for Dad that I can remember. Dad got the first claim on his freshly earned pay. Everything else came second to that. He never needed more than a few dollars, but no matter, he came first at 807.

freedom." No, no, no, Uncle Jay said this too, living in La Jolla where there were many people who demonstrated that, indeed, "money is their freedom."

Try it anyway. You will like it. It does really free you.

Another money saying of Dad's was "Money ain't everything, but it's far ahead of whatever is in second place."

And another one went this way: "Money does not buy you happiness, but it does buy you some really nice things."

MONEY IS YOUR FREEDOM

Dad was famous in the family for his dry humor. It was not always so, as illustrated in this little story. "Money is your freedom" is really a good one to show one kind of humor that he liked.

As I have said, Dad worked for the Santa Fe Railroad Company for many years. Well, one of the perks that a Santa Fe employee enjoyed was something called the pass. This little card allowed both the employees and their families to ride the train on that pass to any place that the line went, and it also allowed them to use other railroad lines too.

The Santa Fe did not know what a mistake it made in giving the Gardenhires the pass. We used it as if it were "our private ticket to ride." We went all over the country and often at the drop of the slightest suggestion of a trip.

I remember that we were having a rather late Friday-night dinner for some reason or other and that the table conversation had hushed somewhat when Mother said, "Let's go to Chicago"—there was a slight pause—"tonight!" Well, we jumped up and cleared the table, packed a few things, and headed for the station. The Ranger left at 9:15 p.m., and we were on it, heading for Chicago. We would spend Saturday night with some relatives who always seemed happy to see us during these "pop calls" amazingly enough. We would take some other train back to Topeka and be back in school, having missed only one-half of one day's schoolwork. It was both fun and very exciting. It took very little money, just some discretionary amount, which we always seemed to have. These discretionary funds symbolized the freedom of which Dad spoke so often to us. It also took a lot of imagination, which Mother had in abundance.

As I said before, we traveled on our pass both together and individually. I used it to go alone to San Diego from Topeka every summer from the time I was eight years old until I was nineteen years old. Well, that is just the beginning of this story.

Neighbors and family and friends often wondered aloud about why Dad took his vacation in two parts: a summer week and a winter week. Most Santa Fe men took their vacations in the summer. But Dad was not one of them. He liked to take us places in winter, and that is just what he did—from Banff to Miami and lots of places in between. Taking us out of school for a week was quite satisfactory for him at these exceptionally happy times.[1]

---

[1] I cannot remember a single time when Dad mentioned "homework" to me or to us. That was something that we just understood to be a requirement for us, so we took care of it without

26

During one such trip to New Orleans, Louisiana, some ancient traveler asked him how he could afford to be taking all five of us on such "a nice trip" in the dead of winter. I overheard Dad laughing as he said to the old gentleman, "Money is your freedom."

As usual, I was underfoot; so when he saw me, he came over to me and repeated the saying to me, "Money is your freedom too, John. With it, you can go places in winter or summer, and without it, you can't go anyplace."

By this time, our house was secure, and Dad had quit his second job. It is interesting that both Dad and Uncle Jay quoted this idea to me over many years. Uncle Jay and his wife, Aunt Bert, took this idea very seriously because they were taking cruises before most folks knew what a cruise was. And when you looked at their home in La Jolla, you knew that they were living their mantra: "Money is your freedom."

Oh yes, another example of this idea shows how Mother used her money in ways that she chose. Whenever Mother wanted to have a day to herself, she would suggest that Ruth and I take $10 and ride the train to Kansas City. Ruth was fifteen or so and I five years younger than she. We would use our famous pass for the train ride to the "Big City" where we would take the streetcar out to Swope Park. Sometimes we would ride the streetcar back and forth to the park, and sometimes we would spend the day at the park. I cannot remember what we did all day there, but we managed to entertain ourselves well enough because every time that Mother suggested a day trip to Kansas City, we were ready and anxious to take that ride. Now that I think about it, our little trips gave Mother and Dad some free time to be together with each other without us being underfoot. I told you that your grandmother was smart! Anyway, had she not had that $10 every now and then, this "downtime" for them would not have happened. So you see, money was her freedom too.

---

instructions or pushes in that direction. They were not necessary, so they were not a part of this equation.

HARDLY EVER IS ANYTHING ALL YOUR FAULT

Have I told you about the Pinkstons* yet? Before I go any further, let me relate one memorable instance of my many encounters with this fateful family.

I came running to the shop where Dad was engaged in some of his many ongoing projects. But as usual, the noise of the place came to an abrupt halt when Dad saw me flying through his open shop door, charging straight for him. He caught me as I screeched to a sawdust-covered standstill, having bumped into him as he moved to dampen the flight of my entrance and kept me from flying on through his work space.

I shouted, breathlessly and loudly, as if his machine were still running. "Daddy, Daddy, Mrs. Pinkston is after me. She's really mad at me! She said that she is going to get me." ** When I was in deep trouble, Dad became daddy to me.

Dad answered me calmly, "What happened?"

I replied, "It wasn't my fault. It wasn't my fault!"

"Yes, John, but 'It wasn't my fault' does not answer my question. Now, what happened?" he asked again.

"Their garage caught fire. And it wasn't my fault!"

"The Pinkstons' garage just caught fire? How? Why?" He wanted to know.

I proceeded to explain that Barbara Jean, Amos, Daniel, [1] and I were making homemade cigarettes and cigars out of newspaper and elm leaves. (The slightest smile made a hint of itself across his face.) Just when we had lit up and were able to keep the light going, Mr. Pinkston came out of his back door and entered his garage. We were sure that he had seen us; so we fled the scene as quickly as feet and legs would allow, dropping our slightly lit, half-lit, as well as fully lit "smokes" where we had been sitting before we were so rudely interrupted. The episode was quickly forgotten as we headed up the alley toward Hancock Street. Soon, we had found other interesting escapades to engage our "loosened" summer afternoon. I told him that I thought no more about the smoking business until I heard the fire engines roaring up Wood Street.

---

[1] Daniel was the Ramey kid who had a bad heart and large purple fingernails. He was not to exert himself; the kids all knew that, but he ran with the rest of us. Oh yeah, he panted a lot.

Suddenly, it all came rushing back to all of us as we saw the leaping flames that the firemen were speeding to extinguish—the flames were something that we were so intimately acquainted with. When the first engine stopped just in front of the Pinkston house, I panicked in the realization of the source of the excitement. As did all of my buddies, I gathered to watch the more-than-efficient firemen extinguish the now-blazing garage.

Once the fire was put out and questions were being asked about how it got started, I attempted to slip quietly away from the still-bustling scene, but Mrs. Pinkston blocked my path. I managed to slip around her broad person and dodged her lunges in her vain attempts to grab me. I flew home with screams of hers ringing in my retreating ears. She was screaming that the fire was all my fault and that I was never to come into her yard again. She was yelling at me, beating the air as if she were striking me, and swearing at me, saying between gasps for air that it was all my fault—a line that she repeated at the top of her lungs.

I was frightened (you can read "scared" out of my swing), and I protested to Dad about the unfairness of it all and repeated through my near-hysterical tears that I was quite innocent. I repeated that I did not do it. I did not do it, I insisted. Smoking was not just my idea! It wasn't all my fault.

Dad put his arms around me and said, "Son, hardly anything is ever all your fault."*

I knew that I was "home free" because anytime Dad called me "son," it meant that his protector mode had kicked in and that he was going to take care of the problem and take care of me too. And that is exactly what happened. Dad went to the Pinkstons' house and talked with several parents including the aggrieved Pinkstons. I heard his telling them that the fire was not just John's doing and that he, Dad, would be responsible for a part of the damage. Things settled down in a hurry after that, and later, I found out why Mrs. Pinkston was so upset. It seems that her new '41 Buick Roadmaster was in the garage, and her husband was in the Buick!

By the way, Dad did not mention the "smoking." He did not have to. And to this day, I do not smoke.

MAKE AND KEEP YOUR FRIENDS

Shirley Richard Gardenhire was one marvelous man, with a twinkle in his eyes and a ready smile, which was often followed by loud laughter.

Another saying that Dad often offered was "Friendship counts for something." And he certainly sold this idea to me by his example, which in his day meant letter writing, not e-mailing. Dad wrote to his friends weekly, and as a result, he had mail virtually every day. And on special days, even the postman would comment on the volume of letters that he received. He corresponded with some friends for more than fifty years. There was an old high school friend in particular who lived in Spokane, Washington, that he loved to hear from and who was the recipient of his regular missives.

By the time he was in his seventies, Dad had left Topeka and was living with Uncle Richard in Seattle. Dad announced very firmly that he was going to go visit this old lady over there in Eastern Washington's Spokane. Of course, that is what happened.

We drove over there and right up to her front door. Heavily, on his cane, he walked up to her rather grand house; and with his cane, he rapped on her door. After a considerable wait, a still-cute, dowager-humped little old lady answered the door; and the first words out of her mouth were "Oh, Shirley, you've gotten old!" They had not seen each other for more than fifty-five years.

Richard and I left them to lunch and visit with each other, and we lunched in beautiful downtown Spokane. Upon our return some three hours later, they were still very deep in conversation.

During our drive back to Seattle, Dad revealed that the little old white lady was his first "squeeze" back in their Alma High School days. This just proved that he lived what he taught. In this case, "Anybody can end a romance with anger and rancor, but it takes a real gentleman to end one so that you remain friends," Dad told us again. His "You really can make and keep friends" ended the discussion that evening, until many miles down the highway toward Seattle, Dad added, "Leave them better off than when you met them."

This is another saying of his demonstrated herein, which took me some years to figure out! But when I did, I found that it works beautifully.

TREAT YOURSELF WELL

One of the sayings that Dad said most often was "Treat yourself well. If you don't, who will?" Well, Dad had no trouble "treating himself well." And he did special things for himself from time to time, like going to see the swallows come back to Capistrano, California, because the nineteenth of March was his birthday; and that day was marked by the swallows' flight pattern. Or he would give himself a special gift, like a new hat that he thought to be particularly smart. Of course, he encouraged us to do the same.

It seems that I have surrounded myself with friends who feel as Dad did. And one wonderfully accomplished person who understood this concept perfectly was my old and dear friend Sadie.

She understood this concept in a clear and practical and tangible regular way—monthly! Sadie had a mantra, and it was "I know a girl named Sadie, and I like her a lot so that I give her something every payday!" Sometimes it was a little something. This "little something" could take the form of a short walk in the park and a smell of the flowers there or even the purchase of bouquets. Sometimes it was a big something that could take the form of a lovely weekend at San Francisco's luxurious Huntington Hotel. Sadie would often say that it was not the purchasing of things that the gate of treating yourself well swung upon but rather upon the conscience's considering and caring for herself—regularly.

Her beautiful large home with its ballroom sat on the western slope of one of San Francisco's finest neighborhoods. Her house and her walled western secret garden (she had two: southern and western) overlooked the Pacific Ocean. When the locals wanted to give a large house party, it was Sadie to whom they went.

Her home was one valued aspect of her world; and she filled it with beautiful, elegant, high-quality new furnishings and exquisite antique pieces. And while fine furnishings and art were her passion, they constituted only a part of her living out her philosophy in life. Much of this "working out" included "the joy of doing something for others." This "doing something" took many forms. One major deed of hers was mentoring, for more than twenty years, two girls for whom, if it had not been for her interest and care (read: money and time spent exposing them to worlds that they would never have known had it not been for Sadie's efforts on their behalf), college would never have been possible. In answer to my question as to why she invested so much in these girls, she said that she got much more than the girls did because seeing them progress made her feel that she was contributing to the future of deserving and talented people, and that made her feel great! Serving those girls was a gift that she also gave to herself. And this gift, she was wont to say, was something she kept giving herself year after year as she witnessed their development, successes, and achievements as they both graduated from college and went on to be examples of refined, competent, responsible, educated, professional adults.

Sadie also led a San Francisco hospital support group for patients with diabetes. The "treat yourself well" part of this work also came from the pleasure that she got from working with these people.

Oh, Sadie had her physical problems; she had severe arthritis that had started crippling both her hands and feet starting early in her thirties and afflicting her throughout her happy long life. Through all of this, Sadie took care of a husband and raised two wonderful children.

While her lovely home was an important element of her treating herself well, as you can see, it was not all that there was to it.

Sadie understood well this idea of "treating yourself well" better than most people did, and we can learn much from her example! Treat yourself well.

STUDY LATIN

Dad was a marvelous "wordsmith" and speller. The evidence for this can still be seen in his letters and other writings. They used to be in a large box in the basement, but they are now in the John Fouts Gardenhire Collection at Spencer Research Library of the University of Kansas in Lawrence, Kansas. He used to have fun by using at least one "new" word in each letter that he wrote. Several of his correspondence buddies did much the same thing, and he would get great amusement out of learning a new word from his friends. This was before television. I learned "terpsichorean," "propaedeutic," and "yerga" from his letters.

Carmen and I had gone to visit Dad when he was living in Seattle with Richard and still churning out letter after letter on his "lap desk" from which he produced all of his missives. I was sitting beside him as he finished up one of his finest pieces. All of us at 807 Wood Street knew that Dad was the best speller in our number. Mother was good, but Dad was better. Yet I wondered why he never used a dictionary. So one afternoon in Seattle, I asked him why he did not refer to the dictionary. Dad replied, "I know Latin, so I do not often need the dictionary. You should study Latin. It would have been better if you had studied Latin when you were younger, but you can still help your English should you choose to do so even now at this very late date." His voice trailed off as if musing on what he was saying. He was teasing me, of course, which was his wont and intellectual game-playing pleasure. This kind of verbal jousting was a real amusement for him and for the rest of us too once we caught on to what he was doing. It was his way of testing us to see if we were paying attention.

So you see that the value of a practical knowledge of Latin provided Dad a lifetime of intellectual stimulation and lots of fun as well. "Study Latin" meant something to us even if only Richard actually took him up on it. His going to Catholic schools helped, but that did not change our awareness and appreciation of the value of it.

KEEP YOUR BUSINESS AT HOME

The "Keep your business at home" saying of Dad's is one that carries a level of embarrassment for me that is quite sharp even until now. Why? Well, with my big mouth, I, having listened to Mother and Dad discuss how much they would be willing to pay for a lot over on the Sunganunga, proceeded to go around my Mud Town neighborhood, telling folks that "my dad is going to buy another lot over on the creek." I said he wanted to have a larger garden spot to grow sweet potatoes, especially since the soil over there was very rich and offered a ready water source. Yeah, you know me. I told it all.

The word—my word—traveled fast and reached one Mr. Baylock who went to Mr. Gaines and offered to buy the same plot, and this happened before Dad had had a chance to speak to the owner about his wish to buy the land. Several days passed during which all of this purchasing activity, unknown to me, was transpiring. I continued blabbing to the neighborhood about what "my dad" was going to do, as was my wont then. No bigger smarty-pants than I existed back then. Of course, when Dad went to make his offer on the plot, Mr. Gaines told him that he had just sold it to Mr. and Mrs. Baylock [1] and at a slightly lower price than Mother and Dad had agreed to offer him. Their price was $300; and the land, one-quarter of an acre, was sold for a mere $275 to an archrival of Dad's.

As I said, it took a few days for the news to completely get around, but get around it did. When I came bursting into the house one afternoon soon after this event occurred, I was greeted by both Mother and Dad who were ready for me with questions

---

[1]   It was the infamous Mrs. Emma Baylock who dipped snuff. This was not thought to be a ladylike thing to do in those days in Mud Town. Dad said that she could "spit around corners." I never did see her do that, but I did see her spit into any one of the several one-pound Folgers coffee cans that she had strategically placed around the rooms in her home. I never saw her miss one single can. Her house was spotless, a fact for which she was famous around Mud Town—no tobacco juice spatters please. Another thing about her housekeeping might also be noted. Her house always had the slightest fragrance of oranges. It seemed that she had developed a process for using the oil of orange peels in her floor wax—Johnson's paste, of course. I remember that her floors had a beautiful and deep shine at all times. Mother said she achieved that high polish on her floors by buffing them, on her hands and knees, every week. In any event, Mrs. Baylock took the cake for being the best housekeeper in all of Mud Town.

regarding how the news of their desire to purchase the said land had reached so many ears and houses in the neighborhood. Did I have anything to do with this spread of their business about the area?

Oblivious to the damage that I had done with my big mouth, I confirmed that I had told folks out of my pride in and excitement over the proposed new land purchase. They were both annoyed and amused with what I had done, spreading their business all over the place. When Mother said that she ought to slap me because of my behavior, I understood more fully the extent of the trouble that I had caused them. I also knew that was not going to happen because Dad was on the scene. She relented, and they proceeded to deal with their annoyance by telling me that whatever was said inside our home was to stay inside. Dad ended their joint lecture to me on this topic with "Keep your business at home." He asked me if I understood that I had made his life a little harder by my talking about our business outside of our house. He had lost an opportunity to get a piece of land very close to our house and which would have been much easier for him to farm than the one that he was forced to buy, which was somewhat farther away from the creek. I assured him and Mother that I absolutely did understand it and that I wouldn't do anything like it again. The guilt here was my own because, as with so many of my mistakes in my youth, he never taunted me or chastised me or belittled me or even mentioned this episode to me again. This last discussion ended with him repeating his mantra "Keep your business at home." That is all that he said on the subject.

YOU CAN ALWAYS COME HOME

I must tell you about this saying of Dad's because it shows so clearly how closely Dad held on to his principles and ideals.

Back during the winter of 1957, Lawrence, Kansas, had a huge snowstorm, leaving ten or twelve inches of the white stuff covering everything. Well, several really smart college boys (I am embarrassed to say that I was one of them) decided to schlep out onto the freshly opened Kansas Turnpike and to block it with county snow barriers. A four-car caravan of KU's best and brightest drove out there and did just that. To our great surprise, we were quickly stopped by the Lawrence Police long before we could make our way back to the Alpha house and accomplish our hoped-for and imagined clean getaway.

Of course, we were not charged with anything since the Lawrence Police did not charge students with anything unless they'd committed a capital crime or some other felonious deed. But our parents were called, and they had to come to Lawrence's city jail to retrieve us before any one of us could be released. Dad was one of the first parents to arrive. He duly signed the stack document of release for me and drove me home to Topeka.

During the entire drive back, he said not a word. When we stepped into the house, Dad only said, "Welcome home, son." And then, as an aside, very softly and almost just to himself, he said, "I thought I was raising an intelligent kid. I didn't know I was raising a stupid child, but . . ." His voice trailed off with a pain and chagrin that I cannot describe; then he added, "Welcome home." He never mentioned the incident to me again.

When I think back to that time, about the self-control that it took for a highly verbal man like he was to remain silent in the face of my profound stupidity, I think that Dad looked awesome to me then; and he still does. He still does.

PLAY RITUAL WITH YOUR PARTNER

I'll tell you how Mom and Dad got along. Their relationship was based on mutual respect and a very private affection for each other, which was fun for them too. They had an ongoing play element in the way they related to each other. They fostered a daily "I'm home" reconnect play ritual that I'll tell you about later.

Remember that your grandparents married at a rather late age of thirty-five. They were tired of living alone and agreed to marry to avoid being in someone's home come the next Christmas, having met at Aunt Ann's Colorado Springs annual Christmas party the Christmas before they got married. You know their story. They agreed to meet in Colorado Springs during the next Easter vacation, which they did; and during that meeting, they agreed to get married. The newlyweds moved to Topeka where Dad had just gotten a new job with the Santa Fe Railroad Company. Five years later, Richard was born. Another five years later, Ruth was born; and five more years later, I was born. All of us were born at home: 807 Wood Street. If you notice a lot of "agrees" in this section, that is because this is how they related to each other. They asked each other if he/she agreed with whatever was going on or being discussed and decided upon. They never did anything that was not the result of their discussion and of their agreeing upon a course of action regarding the issue at hand. There were a lot of "Well, what do you think, old lady/old man?" at the end of any disagreement.

Both Mother and Dad employed a technique of disagreement mitigation at times when some issues had gotten really sharply presented by either of them. What did they do? Well, they quoted lines of poetry that they both knew was a sign that the other one recognized the seriousness of the discussion and at the same time was willing to, if not give in, at least show that he/she was willing to let it go and accept the other's view of the issue. This was true even when one did not agree with the other's view of the issue. Leaving the issue open for more discussion at a later time was a given for them. At these times, Mother would, with a sigh and some hint of laughter in the midst of a hot discussion, say, "OK, old man, 'The road all runners come.'" [1] And Dad might say, "Well, Carrie, 'If there are any heavens.'"[2]

These kinds of exchanges would most often dissolve into their laughing together at whatever was being argued about with a promise that the issue would be revisited at another time. One or the other would get up from the dining room table and depart the scene at this point, and the issue would not be revisited until that other time.

I cannot remember a time when that was not the way that a big, serious, unresolved issue between them got defused and its edges softened somewhat. It is still amazing to me that their arguments always ended in laughter somehow.

Oh, what did they argue about? you ask. Well, one big disagreement concerned the uses of "and" and "or"; another one was over the number of paragraphs an essay should have. You see, they fought over really weighty stuff. These topics were important to them because they both loved language so much. One longitudinal argument between them concerned Latin diction and usages. This one always confounded me because I could not understand any of what they were arguing about. And finally, they argued about the interpretation of poetry, especially Shakespearean verse.

As I look back at the way they related to each other now, it is clear that each considered their relationship more important than any single issue or problem that they contended with. Both Mother and Dad were willing to compromise a position in order to get to the agreement place.

I asked Dad how he viewed their relationship years later after he had left Topeka, and he told me that he and Carrie had a sixty-forty marriage. "When she goes sixty, I go forty. And when I go sixty, she goes forty." Thus, the give-and-take of their marriage was steeped in a balance flowing from their valuing of each other's good judgment and the respect that their connection was based upon.

Dad arrived home from work promptly at five thirty on every workday. Mother had dinner on the table when he hit the door. She did not allow anything to prevent her from having dinner ready for him. She would cut short her phone calls and interaction with us kids to maintain that norm with the presentation of his dinner.

Mother would always be in the kitchen with her back to the porch/kitchen door when Dad came into the house. Upon entering the kitchen, Dad would greet Mother by just saying her name or sometimes by saying "old lady." After one of these announcements, he would amble past her and pat her on her bottom. Her reaction was always the same. She would feign annoyance and say to him, "Get away from here" or "Oh, stop that, old man."

---

[1]   This is a line from A. E. Houseman's poem called "To an Athlete Dying Young."

[2]   This is a line from e. e. cummings's poem called "If There Are Any Heavens." The first line goes, "If there are any heavens / my mother will (all by herself) have one."

Observing this over time, I finally said to Mother, "When Dad comes in and bothers you, why don't you move out of his way so—" I did not get to finish my solution to her problem because before I could do so, Mother snapped, "Who asked you anything about this?"

Who indeed?

BEING "COLORED" MEANS THAT YOU HAVE TO WORK HARDER. SO DO IT

Alissa asked why it is that "we" are expected to achieve what others do by working harder than they do. "It is not fair," she protested. I answered her inquiry with the following saying of Dad's: "Being colored [we were colored in those days], you have to work harder, so do it." Anyway, Alissa, this illustration is both sad and amusing at the same time. My hope is that this kind of thing does not happen anymore. But I am not sure that is the case. What do you think?

One day before KU's classes had begun and after I had enrolled for the new semester, I went home. Dad asked what I was taking, and I happily laid out my schedule on the dining room table for him to examine. While doing so, I complained to him that I had a certain professor who had a wide reputation for not being fair to "us." Expecting a word of comfort or sympathy from Dad, I was startled at what I heard as a fairly sharp response to my complaint. There was not a hint of sympathy in his tone as he said, "Being colored means that you have to work harder to be successful than the other folks. So do it."

Well, with this fresh "kick in the behind," I went back to Lawrence and to my new semester, determined to operate on Dad's newly ordered program; and I did. During the midterm, I got an A from this famous professor at the university. I just knew that I was going to break this old habit for Dr. Funstont.[1]

For some unknown reason, the great man summoned me to his corner office just after the finals had been given and before the grades had been "posted." He sat behind his highly polished but cluttered standard-issue desk and kind of jumped as he observed me entering his office. He greeted me with a low grunt when I said my name. He got right to his point. "Well, Mr. Gardenhire," he announced, holding my notebook aloft and speaking too loudly for the occasion I thought, "yours is the most complete notebook that I have ever seen in all of my years of teaching, but I do not give niggers As."

---

[1]   The university later named a building after this gentleman. How annoying is that?

I was shocked by his candor. But my shock didn't keep me from responding to his stupid racist remarks with my own calm, clear-voiced reply. "Well, you do what you have to do, Dr. Funstont, but you should know that I have just returned from Korea where I killed fourteen Koreans in one afternoon, and I have not forgotten how to do that."

When the good doctor's grades were posted outside of his Strong Hall classroom door a day or two later, there was my A, as big as you can imagine. With "Gardenhire" surrounded by Cs, his list of grades read,

    Garcia, Raul C
    Gardenhire, John A
    Greenlease, Thomas C

On occasion, one who is colored must not only work harder, but he must also help that work along a bit.

This episode did not change by one with the truth of Dad's saying: "Being colored, you have to work harder to be successful than others, so do it."

WHEN YOU HAVE LOTS TO DO, GET OFF YOUR BOTTOM AND GO TO WORK

Do you think that I quoted this saying of Dad's frequently? That is because it represents an attitude toward work that I have experienced the benefit of repeatedly and often. When I went to him complaining about how much I had to do, Dad would say to me, "When you have lots to do, get off your bottom and go to work."[1] And he expected you to "get crackin'" when he reminded you of it too.

When I was in junior high school, I remember asking him how to do that, and he stopped to tell me how to do just that. "Plan your work and work your plan." What a wonderful bit of instruction that was for a fourteen-year-old. He meant that I needed to get organized, and the organization would facilitate the accomplishment of all of the things that I had to do.

Sometimes he would laugh and comment that planning your work prioritize the list of tasks, and when that happens, I would have time to do all of what I needed to do and have time to do what I want to do too. After all, Dad assured me that everybody got the same number of hours in the day. So to him, it was up to me to decide how much I got done. Dad would say, "While you are standing here moaning to me about how 'overloaded' you are with things to do, you could be working on your plan and be out of here by now or sooner, if that is really what you want. You can always tell what is important to you by checking to see what you take care of. If something is important to you, you take care of it. If you don't take care of it, it's not important to you. Testing means thusly you can always tell what is important and what is not important to you and to others as well."

Oh yes, Dad used words like "thusly" and many other multisyllabic terms that he expected us to learn as we heard them and add them to our vocabularies. This we did happily and with fun and pleasure.

When I was drafted into the army, this totally internalized mantra of Dad's served me well. By this time, it was natural and like second nature for me to apply these ideas to the tasks at hand. Well, the military powers that be noticed how efficiently I

---

[1]   Dad would have said "ass."

accomplished my assignments. The result of their noticing my work and their appreciation for my work led them to offer me a chance to go to leadership school after basic training, which I accepted. This added training opened up opportunities for advancement that culminated in my being promoted very rapidly to corporal and, from there, to an assignment with the Fifty-ninth Reconnaissance Company as a company clerk. Typing ninety words per minute helped too! And while this assignment might not seem like much, it meant that I got to stay warm and dry either in a large vanlike truck office or in an office—period. And this was while other members of my company were bivouacked or housed in small tents where it was impossible to keep either warm or dry.

So you see that using Dad's sayings often had immediate and long-term rewards for me in terms of oiling the rails of my life.

NEVER STEP ON AN ANT THAT IS NOT BOTHERING YOU

This saying of Dad's offers us a profound statement of his respect for life. Dad demonstrated this concept of reverence for life as he lived his life. He maintained his position on this subject at all times and without regard for who was there. One instance of his dedication to this principle happened in front of his shop. Mr. Irving and Mr. Ramey (the father of the kid with the big purple fingernails) were standing around the door of Dad's shop, lounging and gossiping, when one of the men shouted, "Damn, man, look at all of those ants!" All eyes were drawn to the thick line of red ants that were making their way from their nest to a food source in our compost pile. Mr. Anderson[1] (at the corner of Wood and Chandler streets in sections so that he, a serious carpenter, could construct a house from that ordered kit)[2] started to kick the line of insects, cutting a footwide swath across the line busy of ants. He was about to kick again, but Dad grabbed him and shouted for him to "cut it out. Those ants have as much right to be here as you do, J. B." Dad said this in a rather annoyed and disturbed tone.

---

[1] Mr. Anderson was a photographer of wide reputation in Topeka and abroad in Eastern Kansas. A black photographer who made a living with photography as his income source was a very rare bird indeed. J. B. was rare for another reason. He built his Cape Cod house from a mail-order kit that Sears and Roebuck had sold and delivered to his lot (at the corner of Wood and Chandler streets in sections so that he, a serious carpenter, could construct a house from that ordered kit).[2] This Mr. Anderson did. And he worked on it every day after work, rain or shine, and during the weekends too. Larger than most other houses in the area, it was a two-storey house in shimmering coats of white paint with two dormer windows in front and one wide triple-window dormer at the back. The Anderson house was the first two-storey house built from the ground up in Mud Town, and it was often held up to Mud Town visitors as an example of what a colored man could do. It is still standing and still quite pretty.

[2] Chandler Street bordered Parkdale Elementary School, which was a block and a half from our house, but we did not go to school there because it was the "white" school. Instead, we went to Washington School, which lay several blocks away, between the Shunganunga Creek on Washington Street. It was so far from home that we had to bring our lunch. Had we gone to Parkdale there on Chandler, we could have come home for lunch.

Dad's comment carried the day because the other men who were gathered around grunted agreement with Dad's position. As they were leaving sometime later, they teased Mr. Anderson about his having kicked the ants for no reason. In mock dismay, shaking their heads and rubbing their fingers together in a shame-on-you mode, they tumbled down our drive, shoving and playfully tussling and poking one another as they left. They headed for Wood Street and then dispersed, going in various directions, both east and west, as they headed home. Dad had made his point to them and to me.

HE WHO DOES NOT ENJOY
HIS OWN COMPANY
IS PROBABLY RIGHT

Dad really believed in entertaining himself. He often said that he was never bored even when he was alone because he could always amuse himself. There were several ways through which he achieved this state of being. Chief among these ways that he managed this state was through were his constant companions—news magazines, newspapers, and books. Dad loved to read and did a lot of reading. He loved the library, which kept him supplied with interesting reading materials. His interests were quite eclectic so that there was always some topic that he wanted to know more about. That kept him with his head in a book.

He had an unusual hobby—that of raising show and sport bantam chickens. His work at raising decorative bantam chickens did engage his time and interest before you could "drop your hat." He had been winning first- and second-prize ribbons at both the Shawnee County and the Kansas State fairs for years. His "birds" won him something every time that he showed them there. For them, Dad developed a feeding regimen that utilized a grain called milo, a feed grain that poultrymen had not discovered as a bird feed quite yet. He studied genetics and worked to breed his show chickens for unusual features like feathered feet and frizzy feathers, as well as unique coloring in feather presentation, especially on the wings where he actually bred a male bluetick with a chevron pattern on its leading edge. This chevron pattern was reminiscent of the chevron pattern now found on the wings of the male Western blue jay. Dad loved his birds and was glad to show them to anyone who just happened to mention the word "bantam" in his presence. At the same time, most of his work with his bantams was done while he was alone.

Are you thinking that the Gardenhires lived on a farm? Well, no, we did not. 807 Wood Street was only eight blocks east of Kansas Avenue, Topeka's main business street (the street of the aforementioned Pelletiers, Crosby Brothers, the Palace, Ray Beers, Harry Endlich, and the rest).[1]

---

[1] Speaking of company, Mr. "Red" Irving, brother of George who cared for Dad's property so well, lived alone and was one of the first folks to buy a TV set. Well, he sat at home drinking

Dad corresponded with his many pen pals. He liked to study Latin. He enjoyed woodworking and had a project in his pipeline toward completion most of the time. So you see that when Dad said, "He who does not enjoy his own company is probably right," he was showing us how to enjoy ourselves when with "your very best company."

Teaching by example, Dad's life demonstrated beautifully how boredom could be avoided. His life was one of engagement, and its example laid out the way to do it.

I applied Dad's ideas about enjoying my own company by doing much of what he did and a few more things besides. I play my piano, memorize poetry, garden a little bit (a very little bit now that bending is more of a challenge than it used to be), engage in touristlike activities. The Bay Area is full of these kinds of things to do.

Alissa, dear, from the letter that you have recently written me, I know that you do enjoy your own company too. I hope that it is the result of what you have learned from all of us, Dad included. In any event, I'll just quote what you wrote.

I supposed I got my love of my own company from observing my parents enjoying their own company individually—you playing the piano or gardening or my mom reading a book or making bread (it was the seventies, you know). This love for my own company was, of course, helped along by my only-child status—having no siblings means you better figure out how to amuse yourself, but for me, it wasn't a hardship. I always answer the same way to those who ask if I miss not having siblings. "No, because I can't miss something I never had." I had a number of stepsiblings and felt the same about them over the years. They're fun to play with, but I'm glad when they or I went home.

I inherited from my parents a love of reading, which was the cornerstone of my foundation as one who enjoys her own company. I read voraciously from the time I learned how to, which was before kindergarten, and thirty years later, I still do. Let me be clear. I read for the pleasure of reading, not to "escape" my aloneness. Reading CAN transport you to another place, but I was just as happy to "come back" and be with you or go outside and play with my friends.

In a word, until recently, most of the things I did I did by myself, and that was OK as I enjoy being with me—I'm very interesting, you know.

Oh! It sounds like you got the idea, and I am glad for you. It is important to have done so, so that you have something to offer in connecting with another person, either casually or more seriously and personally.

---

and watching a "cowboy and Indian" type of show when the "good guy" seemed to be in trouble. Determined to help him, Red ran to his bedroom, loaded his .44-caliber gun, and rushed back into his living room where he shot the villains to pieces. He got along better with his second TV.

DON'T LEND MORE THAN YOU CAN GIVE AWAY

Let me share another money saying Dad had cleverly rolled out at Del Mar's racetrack in the fifties. The saying goes, "Never lend more than you are willing to give away!" Boy, oh boy, what a good idea this is.

We were visiting Uncle Jay and Aunt Bert in their home down in La Jolla, California, when the idea of going to the races came up. Uncle and Auntie were giving us a party to celebrate our arrival. Almost all of the assembled guests expressed interest in going to Del Mar both to see the horses run and to wager on some of the horses. Since the Del Mar trip was an added attraction to the luncheon, several members of the revelers lacked "gambling" money. As a result of that, some folks were forced to rely on the largess of the others in the party whom they "knew" to have money. Travelers, for example. None of this was stated, of course, but it was assumed. And since this happened long before the advent of ATMs, procuring money was done either from the bank or from "walking banks" like Dad. Once the discussion was focused on *the track*, it was quickly decided that the party should jump into their cars and head for Del Mar, which they did. Well, as the races progressed, there were a few winners, but there were a lot more losers among our party. Dad called that fact to my attention by saying to me, "They do not build these hotels down here with winnings. So you better limit your gambling to what you can afford to lose."

One gentleman[1] whom Dad had not known before that afternoon sidled up to him and asked to borrow $25, assuring Dad that he would repay him out of his winnings, or should he not win, he was "good for it" and that he would repay the money the next day. Dad indicated that he would be glad to lend him some money but not the requested amount. Instead, he offered the gentleman $5, which Dad fumbled around in his pocket to find. The man took the money and dashed off to place his bet on the next race. That fellow never saw the silver-dollar money clip that Dad kept in his pocket with its $100 bill around the smaller bills held therein.

Knowing that Dad had a wad of money in his pocket, I asked him why he had refused to lend the whole of the loan amount requested by our friend, and he

---

[1] This gentleman was Otis Fowler, J. Edgar Hoover's summertime La Jolla driver and local summertime lover.

48

turned to me and quoted to me the saying discussed herein: "Never lend more than you are willing to give away." This time, that mantra was accompanied with a quick hug and his trademark quiet chuckle.

During the drive back to La Jolla, he further explained to me that we might leave there and never see that man again, and he did not want to be back in Kansas, angry at that guy over a loan that became a gift. If you lend what you are willing to give away, you don't have to worry about your money in the hands of others. "John, don't you think that it is better for you to have your money and for him to be mad at you than for him to have your money and you to be mad at him? Is there any answer to that question other than 'It's better for me to have my money'?"

BE AT YOUR BEST EVERY DAY BECAUSE YOU NEVER KNOW WHO IS WATCHING

Of the wealth of sayings that I heard from Dad, I learned to apply some to my regular daily living, and you could do so as well to good effect. This idea of being the best that you can be all of the time might look demanding, and it is. But once you've started living your life with this awareness uppermost in your functioning, this saying becomes animated, alive, viable, workable, rewarding, fulfilling, and more. I have a basket full of examples for this saying.

One wonderfully fulfilling example occurred this very summer when the phone rang and it was the voice of a student of mine from 1986 to 1987. She was calling to tell me that my teaching and relating to students were an inspiration to her when she took my English 1A and 1B classes. She related a story of how my stopping at her desk and commenting to her that I liked two aspects of her paper and ending my comments to her with an encouraging word that she had not heard from any other teacher. She quoted me as saying, "Dorene, I expect great things from you this semester. Your paper shows that you can write quite clearly, and that is all that I am accepting from you from this moment on." That little exchange was a change-agent experience for her and quite totally forgotten by me. In fact, I have no memory of that student whatsoever! And my remembering her is not relevant. Doing my best that particular day was, for her, exceedingly relevant.

Being at your best every day affects people in ways of which you have no knowledge. Being at your best can change the course of people's lives and all without you having any awareness of your part in that change. And that is just fine, or maybe that's the way that it should be. Who knows?

That was certainly the way that it was in Dorene's case. That long-forgotten exchange in my classroom had meant a lot to her. It had led her to believe that she could get a master's degree from Sacramento State University, which she did.

Being at your best every day is a powerful idea because it affects lives in ways you know nothing of and that, "change agent like" and even profoundly.

REFUSE TO LIVE YOUR LIFE ON
OTHER PEOPLE'S TERMS

What other sayings did Dad have? Well, I can think of many more, but one very important saying for me is this one. Dad often said, "Refuse to live your life on other people's terms."

Grounded black people do not have to have this saying explained. They know it intellectually, abstractly, theoretically, educationally, as well as experientially and instinctively. That is, they understand this one emotionally in order for them to be grounded in who they are as a black person in this country.

A requirement for blacks is that they utterly understand this saying—concept and all.

"Refuse to live your life on other people's terms." Think about that statement. The statement goes far beyond just don't. It is much more powerful, and thus profound. *Refuse to!* There is a defiant quality undergirding this admonishment. Oh yes, the admonishment part lies there, just waiting to be really comprehended and felt by one who hears this saying of Dad's. When you finally grow to understand and internalize the whole of this saying, you become liberated, free. Free to be the best person that you chose for yourself to be. Getting to this place feels good at the level where, I have been told by many others and from my own experience, I can tell you, opens the human potential to you—your human potential.

Let me tell you about my discovery of the power of this saying for me when I was in junior high school. I got some new jeans, and they were a bit too long so that I chose to roll them up so that the underside of the jeans' legs showed, quite white and vivid. Kids being kids and not knowing what to say about something that they had not seen before, my fellow students began to tease me very nastily. Well, I ran home and told my dad what had happened. He listened to my sad story. The unspoken aspect that I did not understand, Dad explained, was that I was trying to please my new classmates. This was an impossible task, he added, because they did not know what they wanted in the first place and would not know it when they saw it because of that fact.

Did I understand? he asked. Oh boy, did I, especially after he added that there was a difference between fashion and style. "Fashion comes and goes. Style is something that you have, and you have it. Your cuff is proof of it. So why would you want to look like the rest of the kids?" he asked.

51

Dad then suggested that I rethink my wish to look like the rest of them, which I did at that moment. I have not gone back there either.

He told me that a safer path for me would be to choose how I looked and then to "look only like yourself."

Dad said that the kids were pedestrian (I learned that word there and then) in terms of clothes. He asked me why not wear my jeans rolled up and nicely pressed so that the newly created cuff would stay up and neatly at that.

I wore my new creation the very next day to general sartorial acclaim. Soon the vast majority of the jeans wearers were wearing rolled and neatly pressed cuffs too. I had started a fashion trend on the spot.

My report to Dad about this remarkable shift of attitude among my classmates drew a big laugh from him. Then Dad told me to quit trying to please everybody because I could not please them and because they really didn't care, so trying to do so would only keep me miserable as well as waste my time.

Dad ended our discussion with the admonishment: "Refuse to live your life on other people's terms."

He laughed as he added that I would understand it better when I got a little older. He was right about that.

From that time on, I decided that I would not worry about what people thought and to just do what I wanted to do, because as Dad also used to say, "What *they* think does not change the color of ink." That is exactly what I have done all my life.

KEEP YOUR RELIGION
TO YOURSELF

On the subject of religion, Dad[1] was adamant. He believed that it was a private matter and that it should not "leave the house." Dad was annoyed greatly by people who talked about their religion, and he hated those folks who tried to proselytize him or anybody. He often said that doing so was insulting to people as if people could not pick a religion for themselves. He resented those kinds of people whom he was sure were the worst kinds of hypocrites. For those Bible-thumping visitors to 807, he took great pleasure in offering them a drink or something that had alcohol in it like his famous sweet potato cobbler. The partakers would smack their lips and proclaim the wonders of his baking skill and often ask for more. Dad often said that anyone who would tramp around the neighborhood trying to sell their religion made him sick, and he thought they ought to be drawn and quartered. When Mother protested that drawing and quartering were a bit severe, Dad would relent in his outrage and mitigate his position a bit by saying, "OK, honey, maybe the drawing might be enough." They would both have a good laugh at this point.

Dad cited the world conflicts at any one time in history as evidence for the need to keep religion more private. Referring back to wars in ancient times up to wars in his present time, Dad argued that the world would not have so many wars were it not for religion. He would name major wars and cite the religions that fought each other in them. Dad was equipped with lots of examples here because there were so many historical examples from which to choose. History is replete with these kinds of conflicts. He would cite the Peloponnesian War of 431 BC, the Crusades from 1100 to 1300, or the American War of 1812 (these were favorites of his)[2] as examples to make his point, throwing in the Israeli-Palestinian conflict to boot.

Don't look at current times. His argument is made even more cogent and reasonable. Sometimes, when Dad was really pushed on this subject, he would occasionally really irritate Mother by saying, "Religion is the worst idea man ever came up with!" This was a discussion buster! Nothing more would be said on the subject until it came up again.

---

[1] Dad was a Methodist, and Mother was a "holly roller."

[2] It did not matter that some of Dad's examples were not wars of religion. Often, it was the heat and sweep of the discussion that interested him, not the "facts."

SEX AT THE GARDENHIRES

Well, yes, there was sex talk at the Gardenhires, and it was upon Dad where the responsibility of dispensing that subject's how-to and why information fell. His presentation of the mechanics of sex was straight out of the book of anatomy that lay under the stack of reference books in our living room, which I had long ago studied in some detail. This part of Dad's lecture took up a very small part of his lesson on the subject. The moral issues consumed the rest of his presentation. For some reason unbeknownst to me, this lecture took place in his garage workshop, not in the house. In any event, Dad was very uncomfortable when talking about the "how to's" of sex, but he was expansive in talking about the moral issues and the need of our/my responsibility in this part of our/my growing up. His discussions were filled with a lot of "you knows," "its," and a wealth of hand and arm gestures and much gesticulation. And his discussions always ended with his famous saying: "Before you bed down with her, you had better know her kindergarten teacher's name."

When you think about this saying, the complexity and depth of it requires some attention. That is exactly what Dad was trying to achieve with his parenting of us. Thought! I am sure that you can understand the idea of his saying. It asked us to think about what we were about to do and to go into that phase of our lives thoughtfully and with a lot of knowledge and information about our would-be partner. If you know so much about a person to the point that you know about her childhood experiences, it is likely that you will know a lot of other information about that person that will allow you to really be prepared to have sex with that person. This rules out one-night stands. So it might just be that after you know so much about a person, you will rethink the sex and decide that perhaps it is not such a good idea in this instance. You will be much more selective. For sure, Dad's saying put a control on what is too often just a silly and thoughtless act. As we hold Dad's saying in mind, for us, the idea of sex with a stranger is out of the question. Sex would be reserved for someone with whom you have something in common and with whom you are very comfortable.

You will notice that Dad was smart enough to avoid the prohibition of sex. Rather, he just advised that we be very thoughtful about it. As I reflect on his advice, I can tell you that this was a wonderfully good advice, and it served me well. It worked for both Richard and Ruth too. I know because I asked them, and they reported the same thing. His advice saved all of us from making some big mistakes.

At the ripe old age of sixteen and after a little practice with Donna Jean Mason, I was intent on trying out my manhood on Naomi Halfen, a rich Jewish girl whose father hated blacks. Boy, oh boy, was I in love with Naomi! She was not at all pretty, but she was more fun than anyone I had encountered up to that time in my young life. I said nothing to anyone about my feelings or my germinating plan of seduction. It really would not have been much of a seduction because it wasn't required in this instance. Naomi was "crazy" about me and was more than willing to join me in this little escapade.

In any event, Dad must have been a psychic because he noticed and called me into the workshop side of our garage and very quietly admonished me to think about what I was doing. Calmly, he repeated, "Before you bed down with her, you had better know her kindergarten teacher's name." And with an added message as he turned to leave the shop, Dad said, "You know, John, marriage is hard enough without having her roll over and call you a nigger." That ended that! Yet we remain friends, corresponding with each other regularly to this day.

DISCIPLINE YOUR CHILDREN

It seems that there are a lot of "Well, I'll tell you's" in here, but well, I'll tell you what Dad said on the subject of discipline. The one thing that he and Mother did not agree upon was how to discipline us. Of course, we were all quite wonderful children—pleasant, good natured, well behaved, and really cute. So very little disciplining was required for all three of us. But on those rare occasions when discipline was required, Mother and Dad operated on totally different discipline modes. Mother was of the "hit them and forget them"[1] school while Dad was of the "Do not hit my children" school.[2] It is funny, though, that even in this disagreement about discipline, they managed to have an agreement about it. They agreed that Mother would not hit us when he was at home. When there was a problem with one of us that needed their attention and it appeared as if Mother was going to handle it by striking one of us, Dad would stop her by saying to her, "You may not hit my children, old lady." Mother would immediately relent, and some more mild action would solve the problem. This usually took the form of a slow walk to the now-famous workshop where Dad would ask us what happened and whether we understood why he or Mother

---

[1] One time this "mode" did not work too well for Mother. She was at the piano when I walked past her. Well, she swung at me and missed me, throwing herself instead from the piano stool to the floor with a thud. That "swing" redounded to her spraining her shoulder and wrist at the same time. She was weeks recovering from that swat at me, and that event put a damper on her hitting any one of us without cause. When I asked her what I had done to deserve a smack, she said that I probably needed it because I was "always into something." "Due process" was not her strong suit.

[2] I really must add this to the reason that Dad had this aversion for hitting us. I asked him about why he insisted that we not get "beaten up." He told me that when he was fifteen years old, his father attacked him for some small infraction of one of my grandfather's many rules, in this case baking too many sweet potatoes! Well, that beating was so severe and out of proportion with the "crime" that Dad decided during the midst of it that if he were lucky enough to have any children, he would not hit them under any circumstances. His philosophy of nonviolence-laden discipline came out of a conscious decision and while under great duress at that. Was he remarkable or what?

was upset.[3] He always made sure that we knew what the problem was, and then he would ask how we could fix or avoid this kind of problem in the future. He always made us come up with solutions to whatever was the issue, forcing us to think about our behavior. After the discussion, if the issue was major, he would say to us, "Now, I'm going to hit this post, and you had better holler. It'll make your mother feel better." So that was how it went, and indeed, Mother would feel better because I can remember her looking calmer and much less frazzled after one of our trips to the shop.

Oh yes, speaking of discipline, I was given a new red cast-iron dump truck, which I just loved and took everywhere with me about the house. Well, I needed some heavy twine to tie to it so that I could pull it along. Dad had just the thing in the bottom draw of his bedside stand. Happy as a beetle in a pile of dung, I dragged that little truck up and down the drive, which was beside our house. As I passed the open back door, I heard the phone ring; and before it was answered, I overheard Dad say to Mother, "It must be the sheriff calling. Your twine is missing, and you know that he doesn't like people who take things." Neither of them said a word to me about the theft, but every time the phone rang or when someone drove up to the driveway or came to the front door and rang the bell, they would say that it must be the sheriff. They always included some statement of how much they liked me and how much they were going to miss me in their speculation regarding the sheriff too. Needless to say, I put the twine back where I got it, but their speculation regarding the sheriff continued for some time. They did not hit me, but their lesson has lasted a lifetime in me. I did not steal anything until I was in the army many years later and then only because a general inspection was imminent, and some soldier had taken my spotlessly clean and lightly oiled, ready-for-inspection M1A1 trigger housing. And I have taken nothing since!

Discipline, you say? Oh yes, and of the highest and effective quality. You know that because it worked!

---

[3] Dad always allowed us to tell what happened and make what defense of the infraction in discussion as best we could. Even when our "reasons" were pretty flimsy, he would listen to them. Shaking his head at the far-fetched explanations, he would often just laugh at them and then ask us to think of some way to avoid the problem in the future. Discipline with Dad always left you thinking. Dad also counseled against being caught up in the appearance of wrongdoing. To cover this idea, he would say, "Never adjust your hat under your neighbor's pear tree."

ALWAYS BEGIN YOUR ESSAY
WITH AN ADVERB

For Dad's sayings that lay out of the realm of the ordinary, this one does just that. There is an unspoken aspect to this saying. It suggests that Dad was far from the average father in Mud Town who left the education of the kids up to the mothers of the household. On the contrary, Dad was aware of, interested in, and supportive of our schoolwork being completed so that we got the best results for our efforts. This fatherly suggestion came out of his parental concern. It also came out of his own experience, which he repeated regularly and loudly. He began an essay that he wrote back in his high school days with the adverb "traditionally." Dad told of how his English teacher had been so impressed with his essay's beginning that he used Dad's essay as a model for his senior class. Dad was very proud of that achievement. He therefore told us to do as he did with great confidence of that formats' providing us with the same kind of success that he had experienced.

I used his idea on essay beginnings when I studied at the University of Kansas and got the same result as Dad had enjoyed many years earlier. One professor, Dr. McCormic, called me into her office to ask how I had written such a strong essay. I did not tell her that I was using a formula that my dad had taught me at the dining room table of our Mud Town home. The adverbial first word and the five-paragraph essay that Mother and Dad argued about worked just fine for me.

This technique served me very well later when I worked on my master's thesis. I made a point of using the adverb to start my thesis. I can tell you that it was received with much enthusiasm by my committee, and my "traditionally" carried the day there too. What fun that master's degree defense of my research was! The committee could hardly get past the first page of my thesis. Their discussion of my paper became a discussion of the "style" of the writing rather than a detailed review of my research. As interesting and amusing as their comments were, I was a little annoyed at them because I was more than prepared to talk about my research, which I believed to be important to the well-being of the college where I worked. They finally got to my research, but my hour was almost up by the time that they got to it. No matter, I was prepared, and that is what was important to me at that time.

WHEN SHOPPING, ALWAYS BUY THE BEST

Dad's "When shopping, always buy the best" was more than a slogan to him. It was a way of life for him. If you remember that Open Road Stetson hat story, you will have a hint of how serious he was about buying the best and what he would do to have the best. That represents just one example from a list that would be too long for this discussion. Take his insistence on driving a "fine car." Dad bought either Cadillacs or Packards, not in that order, but those were his choices of automobiles. Dad wanted the best of the models available, so he kept a Fleetwood after the Packards were no longer produced. He liked the large trunk of that model, saying, "I can always toss a couple bale of hay in the trunk of a Fleetwood." That was a joke, of course, because he had no hay to toss into the trunk of anything. Oh yes, and Dad wanted a new car every three years. He never bought used ones because he didn't want to sit on any "farted-over cushions."

When it came to clothes, only the best would do for him, so he shopped at the two best men's clothing stores in Topeka: Ray Beers and the Palace. He passed his attitude on to me early on in that he allowed me to shop at the Palace on my own when I was only twelve or thirteen years old. I could buy anything that I wanted and did so just signing Dad's name. I still have a cashmere sweater that I'd bought there when I was in high school. Shoes—did someone say shoes?[1] Dad's dress shoes were of fine English brands called McAffee, Baker, as well as of good old American brand called Florsheim. Sometimes he bought a pair of Nunn Bush shoes, which were very god shoes in those days. Dad had a pair of "good" dress shoes. He had a pair for each suit that he wore.

I got his appreciation for fine shoes while very young, and I was abetted in this interest by my dear uncle and aunts in La Jolla. When they discovered that I had

---

[1]   Every Saturday evening, each of us would put the shoes that we were going to wear to church the next day on the back porch. Dad shined all of them for us. He insisted that our shoes be well polished, including the backs and heels. "If a man won't shine the backs and heels of his shoes, he will not wipe his ——," Dad always said.

Of course, I did not want that reputation, so I carefully polished my shoes front and back—even to this day! This instruction of Dad's paid off nicely for me when I was in the army. There, I always got plus gigs on my shoes and boots for their highly polished front and rear.

never had a pair of shoes made just for me, Uncle Jay and Aunt Bert took me to Stewarts in the village there and had a pair of bench-made, square-toed black-and-white Italian shoes ordered and made for me. They were soft as butter and very beautiful, and I wore them for more than fifteen years. Oh, I was all of fifteen years old at the time.

It gets worse. Upon my retirement from teaching at Laney Community College in Oakland, California, I gave away over thirty pairs of my little friends, Salvatori Faragamos, Ballys, Giorgio Brutinis, Alfanis, Pepe Albaladejos,[2] and more.

For Mother and Ruth, the same rules applied. Their stores were Pelletiers, Crosby Brothers, and Harry Endlich. If there was some special occasion that demanded something unique and elegant, it was to Harry Endlich that they went.

Now, when it came to other kinds of items—take, for example, our kitchen appliances—it was the same. The top-of-the-line adorned our kitchen: a Chambers range, a Servile gas refrigerator (yes, gas, and I do not know how it worked either, but it did and very well at that), a Hamilton gas clothes dryer when no one on Wood Street had a dryer, and Masonite countertops. Having new products first amused Dad a lot. At the time when Mud Town folks were just discovering silver plate flatware, we had in our dining room buffet drawer a beautiful Wallace Sterling service for eight in their grand baroque pattern. Talk about something that both Dad and Mother were proud of, and this service was it.

This "beat" goes on.

Are you asking how Dad could afford all of this stuff? Well, you remember that job at the Santa Fe Railroad Company? That job of a "mechanic" paid considerably more than the ordinary railroad "grunt" job paid. The Santa Fe attempted to pay the black workers less than it had paid the white workers whom Dad and the other black men had replaced. The courts would not allow them to do that. And as I told you earlier, Dad worked a second job for several years, and some of the money he'd earned was used to fund this rather mildly grand lifestyle.

He also had in my mother a master money manager. She could have run the country, and Dad often complimented her on her skill. They saved for large-budget items and ran no accounts beyond a month. I don't know how they did it either, but they did it.

"Always buy the best," Dad told us often enough for me to believe him. "Good stuff looks better and lasts longer. So it is cheaper in the long run," Dad always said. These were the reasons that he gave for shopping as he did.

---

[2]   These are (I still have them) gorgeous light tan wingtip Spanish oxfords, and I had been wearing in New York recently when hailing a cab. The elegantly attired lady who alit from the same cab saw them and exclaimed, "Great shoes!" I replied, "Thank you! Madrid, 1984." Remember, always go to Spain in August because all of that leather is on sale in August.

ALWAYS COMPLIMENT A BULLY

If there ever was one of Dad's sayings that worked, it is this one. Back in junior high school, I found myself suddenly faced with some taunting that I had never experienced before. Even though I had friends who supported me quite thoroughly, an overgrown kid named R. L. Steel[1] became my nemesis for some reason known only to him. Now, I had known this kid all of my life since his family lived less than a block from us, and I could see their house from my bedroom window. His was a large family with fourteen or fifteen kids running around over there in their house. There were, in fact, so many kids that the parents stopped giving them names and instead just gave the last six or seven of them initials such as C. W., H. D., D. S., and L. D. L. D. was in my class, and I knew and liked her. R. L. was one of the last six or seven, of course. Well, as I was saying, he began to tease me about my newly gained weight,[2] which I tried to camouflage with a blue sweater that hung loosely about my now-too-rotund body. It did not work. R. L. noticed and commented to me about it. "Fat Ass" and "Uncle Pudge" were two of his favorite terms for me. I responded with

---

[1] R. L. did well. He became a very successful attorney in spite of having grown up very poor. And I mean poor! The Steels were so poor that unlike the rest of Mud Town that burned either wood, like we did, or coal to heat their houses in winter, they burned discarded, broken old automobile batteries that his father gathered from auto repair shops and gas stations. Their house always smelled of burning rubber, and so did the Steel kids in cold weather. They were clean enough, but the odor of the space heater ruled. The Steel diet was also rather limited. They ate lots of fried potatoes, fried in a huge iron skillet atop the front room space heater and not in their kitchen. They could not afford fuel for both stoves. I remember watching Mrs. Steel prepare this dish; and the ingredients included sliced irish potatoes, chopped wild onions, salt and pepper, bacon, or other meat fat drippings. These items were fried to a beautiful brown crust and served with hoecakes and bowls of hot sweet-corn husk tea. These fried potatoes were the best that I ever ate. Oh yes, I did eat over there once, and Mother had a fit about it. She scolded me, saying that the Steels were not able to feed another mouth "poor as they are" and that I should stay away from there at suppertime.

[2] The cause of my weight gain was my discovery of peanut butter. Mother would not buy it because she thought that it was "low-class food." So I had to purchase it in small jars and eat it surreptitiously. This I did until my rear end was wide enough to show a wide-screen film on. It took years for me to outgrow this craving and the fat that it spawned.

my own retorts regarding the weight of his mama (you know, the Dozens, a verbal game, played quite fiercely back then) as long as I was in my group, of course. I was mad, but I wasn't a fool!

I was leaving the south door of East Topeka Junior High School after school on this day, happily tooling toward home, when R. L. caught up with me and my small circle of friends. He passed us, turning to toss his barb of the afternoon. All at once, he stopped and confronted me much more closely than my comfort would allow. I thought that he was going to hit me, so I stepped back. In that moment, Dad's saying flashed across my mind like a subtitle screen at the opera. "Compliment a bully," it said, and so I did. Loudly, I said, "Great haircut! Who cut it for you, Jellyroll?"[3] R. L. stopped in his all-too-worn shoes as if he had been frozen in time. His mouth was working, but for a very brief moment, nothing came out. Finally, he stammered out, "Thanks, man. Mr. Harris." R. L. whirled around and continued running toward home ahead of me and my buddies. "Compliment a bully" impressed R. L., and from that day on, he became my main defender throughout the rest of my Topeka school years. Of course, I did not know that I needed defending. Somehow, he and Darrel Peyton did. Darrel's taking on this role resulted from his having lived next door to my cousins Vassie and Walter Gardenhire out there on Western Avenue.

In high school, years later, I overheard R. L. in conversation with a bunch of "toughs," saying something to the effect that they had better not mess with John Fouts (that is what I was called all through high school because there were so many Johns that each of us was called by our "John" and our middle name) because John was his friend. Even this bunch knew what that meant.

"Compliment a bully!" Well yes!

I wonder how Dad knew that. I never did ask him about it.

---

[3] Jellyroll was the nickname of Vernon Fox, Dad's very best friend and a fellow Cadillac man from his heart.

BE SATISFIED ONLY WITH THE BEST WORK THAT YOU CAN DO

Now, this saying of Dad's is one that we heard all the time. It did not matter whether it was as simple a task as emptying the wastebaskets around the house or a more demanding chore. Dad was there with this mantra: "Be satisfied only with the best work that you can do."

I recall one instance when Dad stopped me as I was doing my chore inside the house. My chore was keeping the wastebaskets empty and clean. Well, Dad spied one piece of paper at the bottom of the back hall's basket. Needless to say, I had not noticed it and was on my way to replacing the basket as I prepared to head for the next basket, which was in Ruth's bedroom. Halted in my tracks by his "Young man"— meaning me, of course—I answered him. "Sir?" I responded as I turned to face him. "Are you finished with this basket? I hope not because it is not empty. Come here and look for yourself," he said, holding the basket up so that I could look into it as he spoke. I sheepishly looked, and there at the bottom of that basket was the biggest piece of paper on the planet. At least that is the way that it looked to me at the time. I reached for the basket; but he took my arm and stopped me, saying to me, "John, be satisfied only with the best work that you can do, not half do."

Dad went on to explain that doing a job well allows you to be happy with it and know that everybody will be happy with your work. He told me that this might not seem important now, but it would be good to remember when I would be working at a bill-paying job. He told me about his boss who was a man who wanted to find fault with his work because he did not believe that a black man could do the "railroad car truck" repair and replacement job. He described how he had worked hard to learn how to do the difficult and dangerous work safely and well and how he, through hard work and study, had mastered the job so well that it was he to whom foremen came when they had repair problems in all of the shops. He said that it did not happen in a vacuum. It happened because of his determination to do the best job that he could. The result was that his boss had no choice but to recognize his excellent work whenever he had to ask for help or needed advice on some repair. That was how it was when his boss had to tell anyone about the work that Dad performed. But it was a different story in his written reports on Dad. It turned out that years later, Dad had an occasion, upon his retirement, to see his evaluations.

This very same boss had written Dad up so that his record was so bad that on paper, Dad looked like a totally incompetent worker who needed constant supervision for him to function at all, even in the simplest work. Dad was shocked by what he read, and I can remember his saying to Mother, "With this kind of record, how did I keep a job?" Chuckling to himself as he gave her a quick hug, he said, "They knew that this evaluation stuff was all lies."

Pay attention. "This is good stuff" (quoting Aunt Anna as she described something she had cooked).

Keeping Dad's saying in mind, I applied it to my work every day. And it worked too. My working to serve my students so that they would achieve at their best was demonstrated semester after semester when my students were able to show the greatest reading-level development than any other teacher's students in Laney's English Department. My incorporation of Dad's mantra into my job was shown by my Teacher of the Year Awards several years consecutively.

"Be satisfied only with the best work that you can do."

Thanks, Dad. You were right!

IT'S A POOR DOG THAT
WON'T WAG HIS OWN TAIL

"It's a poor dog that won't wag his own tail," Dad often said of himself especially when he was questioned about his readiness to talk of his own abilities. To him, this was not braggadocio at all but rather a recitation of what he knew his skills and abilities in any particularly area to be. His report here was more of a listing of items on a bulletin board of "can do's."

One glorious Kansas winter morning—brimming with cold, wet, heavy snow, and winds that blew long coats horizontal—Mrs. Mary Allan appeared and was almost blown through our front door. She was there to ask if Dad could be "in charge" of the fast-approaching Men's Day activities at Mt. Olive United Methodist Church [1] where Dad was not only a member but a also "deacon." She was looking for someone to supervise the whole fund-raising and celebration-filled day. I liked Men's Day because Mr. Burnette always made his wonderful big biscuits.

As soon as her request had been stated, Dad, in short order, presented his list of qualifications. It was as if he had been expecting to recite his readiness to lead the men on their day. Dad knew all of the men in the church. He knew what experience these men had during "our day's" activities in the past years. He had sources for the food. He had sources for the supplies that would be needed to present and serve the luncheon that always followed the morning service. He could obtain these cheaply because he knew the supplying merchants. He could delegate to just the right men particular tasks since he knew just what each one of them could do best. He could get free advertisement in the *Capital Journal.* He was experienced in selling ads in the program that they would produce. He could get it printed. He

---

[1]   As a very little kid, Mt. Olive always presented a challenge to me when I was made to go there because it had a great crack in the ceiling that I was sure was going to fall at any moment. My way around that was to cower in the side of the sanctuary, hoping that it wouldn't fall on me. Of course, I never told anyone about my fear; and as I grew older, I realized that the old crack was there to stay, partly because no amount of fund-raiser had cured the problem and partly because it got to be fun to watch it as it grew ever so slightly with each passing year. The crack was still there when we held Dad's funeral in Mt. Olive many years later.

could handle the city parking permit to cover short-term double parking there on Twelfth Street. He could do it all with alacrity and élan, Dad assured her.

Mrs. Allan left, convinced that Dad was the man for that leadership-laden job and said as much several times as she was blown toward her "step down," low long maroon-and-cream Hudson sedan.

Dad had the job.

Mother feigned annoyance at the performance that she had just witnessed and commented to Dad, "Well, Daddy, you sure laid your stuff on her!" In mock ignorance of what Mother was talking about at first, Dad laughed, gave Mother a quick hug, and said in a stage whisper, "It's a poor dog that won't wag his own tail, Carrie!"

YOU ARE NOT BETTER THAN ANYONE, BUT YOU ARE JUST AS GOOD AS EVERYBODY

Alissa, you once asked how we dealt with the segregated Topeka world, particularly where the schools were concerned. I said to you, "That's a really wonderful question, honey. I'll tell you about my first experience with 'desegregated' schools." I'll note that two of Dad's sayings guided me through the process mightily, though. In mildly segregated Topeka, the black students studied at all-black schools from K through sixth grade. At the seventh grade, all Topeka students—black, white, and others—were thrown together in what was then called junior high schools, serving seven to nine years of instruction leading to and through the twelfth grade at Topeka High School. THS was the place everyone went since it was the only high school in town unless, of course, you were Catholic and went to Capital Catholic or unless you chose to go there for some reason like the reason that Dad sent Richard there.

While shopping for Richard's tenth-grade books, Dad noticed that the books that he and Richard were being offered were not only badly used but they also differed from those being offered to the white tenth-grade shoppers.

Dad stormed out of that bookstore and drove directly to the Catholic high school. The nuns welcomed them warmly and enrolled Richard immediately.[1] Richard's six feet two inches and one hundred and seventy-five pounds did not hurt his application one bit. The Catholic high school's athletic director did not let them get to the car before he had assured Dad that he had personally "taken care of

---

[1]   It was not only the nuns who welcomed Richard at Capitol Catholic, now Hayden High. Those white girls were just delighted to have him there. The telephone started ringing at 807 so that soon he got his own phone line. Oh, he had to pay for it but that he could take care of because the coach had gotten him a little "job" that paid him some pocket money. At Richard's fiftieth high school reunion, one of these gals spotted him entering the reunion hall and charged over to him, hugging and kissing him. He did not recognize her for the longest time, but finally her name came to him, and he blurted out to her, "Oh, Joan, what are you doing now?" She replied, "I'm a governor."

Richard's processing." A vision of basketball and football championships danced in the director's eyes, you may be sure.

As for my own experience with that transition from segregated to desegregated education, I had a ball! The reason for the ease with which I made that supposed leap was that I had heard Dad saying repeatedly, "You aren't better than anyone, but you are just as good as everybody," and I believed him. And the consequence of my belief was that I was not intimidated by "the competition." What competition? I soon discovered that I was as well or better prepared than any kid in my new class. On top of that, I made friends instantly.[2] Some of those kids I'd made friends with I am still in contact with some fifty-nine years later and counting. Several of these friends were pure-gold people and remain so. I loved at least one or two teachers from every grade there at East Topeka Junior High School. Teachers love good students. I know that from listening to Mother's teacher friends who lunched at the house occasionally. They joyously talked about some really outstanding students that they had enjoyed working with or with whom they were now working.

I did my work at East Topeka Junior High School for another reason, and that was because I had often heard Dad declare that "blacks have to work harder to be successful, so do it." He was right on that count, as he so often was, so work I did and quite happily so. Being really smart did not hurt either!

Oh yes, Alissa, there was another more subtle unspoken reason for my diligence during that period, and that was the hushed competition among the fathers of the junior high kids, most of whom worked at the shops of the Santa Fe Railroad Company. You see, I wanted to make my dad proud of me. My sparkling grade cards just filled him with pride. His pleasure at my having done well was enough for me.

So you see, dear, confronting Topeka's desegregation bugaboo did not pose a trauma for me in any way. For me, it was not much of a challenge, and it really was quite a lot of fun, mostly because I could hear Dad's various mantras: "You are not better than anybody, but you are just as good as anybody" and "Blacks have to work harder to achieve success, so get to work!" For us, it worked.[3] There is wonderful security in being supported by those whom you care about.

---

[2]　Keith Schulte, Joleen Knapp, Bob Soucy, Richard Duran, Ethel Carrol, and a handful of others proved be "pure gold" people then and remain so until now.

[3]　It did not just work for us; it worked for the vast majority of Mud Town kids. The success stories from that little area are impressive: teachers, professors, college presidents/chancellors, superintendents, nurses, military brass, legislative representatives, bank presidents, CEOs, attorneys, entrepreneurs, dentists, physicians, and more. Nobody went crazy, and nobody went to jail. They all did well or very well. Why? Well, we all came from "intact families," and we had teachers who cared about us and often told us so. Oh, and all Mud Town adults took responsibility for us so that we felt safe and cared for.

ALWAYS TAKE CARE OF YOUR PETS

Dad loved his birds and his dog. We kept a pet dog for all of my young life in Topeka. The first one that I can remember was Butch. He was a large bluetick coonhound who had a big sound to his bark, but he was just that—all bark and no bite. In fact, he thought that he was a lapdog and loved to come into the house on rare occasions and sit with his foreparts on the lap of anyone who would allow him to light there. You can see why he was not often in the house, but on really cold days of winter, Dad would let him come in for a brief time. He really led a very comfortable life outdoors. He had a cozy, carpeted, clean doghouse, which was built next to our back porch and which was protected from the cold north wind by both its walls and by its placement itself. Dad built it so that the back and side walls were against our house so that there was a kind of mild heat source warming the back and sides of Butch's house.

I remember a very cold, fiercely wind-driven blizzard of a storm that left a foot or more of snow with drifts that were considerably deeper than that covering the yard and the driveway. Butch's house was buried under great piles of freshly drifted snow. After breakfast, neither Ruth nor I made a move to go out and feed and water Butch. We were too comfortable lounging in the kitchen and so warmed by the heat of the oven that had just disgorged some of visiting Aunt Maude's morning partylike orange biscuits. (The recipe is in my cookbook.)

I do not know what we thought that poor Butch was going to do that morning, but we did not get a chance to explore that subject because Dad addressed it without asking us that question. He got up and went out to see about the dog. And this was before Dad went off to work. Dad wrapped up and strode outside to shovel the snow away from the doghouse and put fresh, warm water just inside the entrance. Dad came back into the house, got some scraps from our breakfast, and added some dry dog food to it. He made a second trip out there and fed the dog. When Dad returned from his second trip, he asked why neither of us kids had made a move to care for the dog.[1] We

---

[1] By this time, Richard had gone off to become the first black V-12 Navy trainee from Topeka. He discovered that the test for the V-12 college training program was being given at his high school, but the powers that be decided that Richard could pass the test, so they did not tell him about the test. He stumbled upon it by pure chance, went in, and took the test. He received one of the three or four best scores on the test as given at Capitol Catholic High School that spring. Surprise!

all had excuses, chief among which was the inconvenience of going out in the cold to take care of Butch. He was not amused and said that the dog had not chosen to live with us, that we had chosen the dog, so it was our responsibility to take care of him, inconvenient and uncomfortable as it may be. Dad ended his speech with the comment that said we needed to always take care of our pets because they could not take care of themselves. "You picked him. He didn't pick you. So when you see his needs, get on it!"

From that time on, the "postman's slogan" preceded our going out to care for our dogs, from Butch onward. **[1] That would include Rex and Captain Billy,[2] a purebred cocker spaniel with lovely brown-and-black markings and floppy, hairy huge ears. These wonderful spaniel trademarks housed whole committees of fleas who lived quite happily ensconced therein. They required careful treatment from time to time, especially in the summer. Well, after this "take care of your pets" speech, neither of us had to be told again to get busy and take care of Billy's flea-laden ears. We got that lesson well learned. We even learned to enjoy pet caregiving, and the dog benefited from our learning.

This saying of Dad's is still in place with us. Ruth has a cat that lives in the "lap of luxury." And I noticed that your cat, Alissa, lives pretty well too.

---

[1]

[2] Captain Billy was a very smart dog. In fact, he was smarter than some of my relatives. Remember, Alissa, when you and a few of your friends came running into our backyard where I was working on some gardening project, exclaiming that "Captain Billy is riding the 'kick and go'"? Finding that announcement hard to believe, I'd said to you that a dog could not ride a scooter. You insisted that the dog was riding the toy scooter and pulled me to the front of our house to witness it for myself. Sure enough, Captain Billy was riding the thing; with his forepaws on the handlebars and with his left rear paw on the deck, he pumped smoothly with his right rear paw and glided up and down the street, just as straight and as smoothly as a child could do. Captain Billy could indeed ride the "kick and go." We should have taken a picture of him and sent it to *Ripley's Believe It or Not.*

ALWAYS CLEAN UP
YOUR OWN MESSES

This saying can be illustrated with a very short example. "Clean up your own messes" was demonstrated by Dad every time he left his now very famous shop. Whenever he left the shop for the day, he swept up any shavings or sawdust or any other kind of debris that he found on the floor of his workspace. I remember one time when Dad and Mr. Harris were about to go to Sedalia, Missouri, to buy sorghum.[1] Dad had gotten a very early start on his work in his shop and was ready at 9:00 a.m. to go as he had promised that he would be. Mr. Harris appeared at the appointed hour and was anxious to go, shouting over Dad's noise as he bent over the job in progress there. "Come on, Shirley, let's get on the road!"

Dad stopped immediately, but rather than dashing out as Mr. Harris expected him to do, he grabbed his broom and started to quickly sweep up the workroom leavings. "I always clean up my own messes" was all that he said then to an impatient Mr. Harris. But as Dad got into Mr. Harris's shiny green-and-white Ford pickup truck,[2] he said to him, "See, Sam, the road to Sedalia is still paved."

---

[1] Sorghum is a delicious Western grass product that tastes like something between molasses and cane syrup. Dad bought gallons of the stuff for our winter's sweetening needs. It went into all kinds of dishes—cakes, pies, pones, ice creams, puddings, hot winter cereals, and more. Dad whipped sorghum together with soft butter for use on biscuits or pancakes or waffles for breakfast, which Dad cooked for us every Sunday morning.

[2] He kept that pickup waxed and clean as other people kept their automobiles. His was the only pickup truck that I knew about back then or today even with whitewall tires.

READ THE NEWSPAPER

I can tell you a little about this saying of Dad's, and it is mostly from my observation and an occasional statement: "Read the newspaper." Dad loved the *Kansas City Star*, which we took in the Sunday edition only. This issue Dad read from cover to cover. My most vivid memory of Dad and his newspaper reading remains in the form of a kind of ritual of spreading the *Topeka Daily Capital* out on the dining room table before he went off to work. I can still see his wide (Dad stood six feet and four inches tall and weighed two hundred and thirty pounds) coveralled self bent over the paper as he leafed through it, skimming the contents, before he dashed off to join his ride. If his ride was not there by 7:30 a.m., he would either drive himself to work or he would have Mother drive him should she have need of the car that day. Either way, he was never late for work, a fact of which he was quite proud all his life.

Dad encouraged us all to read the paper because he liked being full of information and assumed that the rest of us kids felt the same way. He was right about me in that regard, but Richard and Ruth were a little less excited about it at that time. Out of respect for his thoughts about the subject, they kept that bit of information to themselves.

If he was reading a long article that he was interested in but did not have time to finish it before he headed out for work, he might say to one of us to read it and tell him about it when he returned. This happened quite often, and I now think that it was his way of getting us involved in the reading of the newspaper.

You might also include the magazines such as *Time* and the *US News & World Report*. Dad read them both and would suggest stories and articles for us to read as he did with the daily paper. This took on at least one of us. When I was visiting Ruth the last time, I noticed that she subscribed to both *Time* and the *US News & World Report* even now. Dad would be proud of her.

I did see the effect of this newspaper reading once in Dad's case. He and Mr. Mayhue[1] were deep in discussion of the hazards of deep mining of coal. The

---

[1]   Mr. Mayhue was the same gentleman whose screen door Richard had torn off while dashing around Mud Town, announcing that I, his new baby brother, was born. He was also the one who ate the whole of Aunt Maude's chocolate pie. It seemed that he was left alone in our kitchen to wait for Dad to return from some errand or other. Well, while he waited, he tried a teeny piece of Aunt Maude's chocolate pie, which was cooling on the kitchen table. The

discussion hinged upon the kinds and dangers of poisonous gasses found deep underground. Several men were on the Harris's back porch, and not one of them could name the gas that was so deadly to the miners. Dad came up with methane, which, I am sure, he discovered in the paper only a few days ago because I, at his suggestion, read the very same article. The men gathered were totally awed by Dad's expertise and agreed all around that "Shirley sure knows his stuff."

So now, I am sure that you see the wonders of newspaper reading, so "read the newspaper."

---

look of Aunt Maude's beautiful pie was too much for the man, and so he kept eating one piece after another until the whole thing was consumed. When Dad returned, Mr. Mayhue just said, "Tell Maude that when she makes this pie again, she better make two!"

BE ON TIME

Well, friends, on the question of time management, Dad was adamant. "Be on time!" Dad insisted whenever we went anyplace. And it did not just apply to going places. He meant it to apply to lots of things, chief among which was being on time for school and for having schoolwork finished and turned in on time. This also included his being on time for work, especially. Dad was never late for work in more than thirty-six years at the Santa Fe Railroad Company shops. Many times during the winter, when crosstown travel could be a problem, Dad left an hour early so that, should the roads be impassable, he could walk to work. As a result of his penchant for punctuality, Dad saw to it that the Gardenhires were the first ones to arrive at events and that we were on time for everything. We were famous for that in Mud Town. Of course, there is an exception to this rule in every family, and Uncle Charlie[1] held that spot. All of his sisters and brothers proclaimed, with hands in the air, that he would be late for his own funeral.

---

[1] Uncle Charlie had the most memorable wake of all the wakes that I can remember or that I ever heard told, as Topeka wake stories go. His wake remains so vivid in my mind because of the exuberance of the friends and family who kept vigil at his wake. In those days, the undertaker brought the body to the house the evening before the funeral. Once the casket had been arranged in our living room, the party began. There were lots of wonderful food. The table just groaned with the weight of the variety of dishes offered by those who came to Uncle Charlie's wake. There was a vast quantity and variety of liquor too. Kansas's being "dry" did not mean a thing to this crowd. As the drinks were consumed and the food eaten, the revelers began to stand and tell stories about Uncle Charlie. The deceased lay there, looking very grayish in his powdered and dead way. At least that was how it looked to my nine- or ten-year-old eyes. As the night progressed, the party got more animated as the storytellers began to dance around the coffin. Suddenly, my "well lit" cousin Walter Gardenhire fell into the coffin and knocked it off the crepe-paper-draped sawhorses, which had been commandeered from Dad's shop. The head end of the coffin fell to the floor with a great thud. Uncle Charlie slid half out of the thing and lay with his arm all up in the air in an odd fashion. The excitement and fun of that spill washed over the folks in the room. There was a swirl of folks laughing, shouting, and singing as they tried to set the horses back in place and returned the coffin to its rightful position of honor on them. The problem for them was that the gang there could not get Uncle Charlie's arm to lie flat beside his body in the way that Mr. Bowser had positioned it when the casket was opened earlier in the evening. After many attempts to

74

He was not. That was a big joke around the house. From it I learned how valuable having a reputation for being on time could be when several of my jealous and small-minded colleagues complained about me to Fred Finch, the principal of McKnight Junior High School. Calmly and patiently, Fred listened to their carping and ended his meeting with us by saying, "John is on time for class, better than all of you. That shows me that contrary to the stories that you have been telling me, John's punctuality belies all of what you have said. His being early to work demonstrates to me that John Fouts is very interested in what we are about here at McKnight. It also tells me that John supports our mission very strongly. Now, let me recommend something to you." To Fred's way of thinking, being on time meant dedication and interest in the work. That can be true, and in my case, it was very much the case.

And I will tell you of the advantage you gain from doing your school papers better than "on time." Turning papers in early makes the teacher believe that you are really interested in the course, which is always a plus; and should you need to improve the paper in some way, you will have time to do so before its deadline. When I was in school, I made a habit of treating my papers that way, and it worked beautifully for me.[2]

Another example of the value of punctuality happened during my army years. By now, it was second nature for me to do things on time so that the army inspections were easy for me. I took care of army demands as assigned and never let them pile up, as did many of my fellow foot soldiers. Rather than working half of the night away in preparation for an inspection, I was famous for going to bed while the rest of the troop toiled away, doing the marking of new equipment that they should have done as soon as that equipment was issued to them.

Be on time and stay on time. It works!

---

get that arm to lie in the right position, they just gave up and remained "in tears" with laughter until time for the funeral the next morning. When Mr. Bowser arrived to remove Uncle Charlie and take him to Mt. Olive, that arm was still sticking up out of the casket, and the ones who were still at the wake were still laughing about that arm and about the wonders of Uncle Charlie's wake. When Uncle Charlie's casket was opened for viewing of the body for the last time there at the church, that arm popped right up again; and the fun of it ensued all over again, right there in Mt. Olive Church. I'll tell you that I shall never forget Uncle Charlie's wake.

2   One Dr. Gilbert, a terribly walleyed Kansas University professor of Italian renaissance history, was so impressed by my habit of early paper submission that he called me into his office to offer me a slot in their history-major grant program, thinking that, because of my pattern of paper offerings, I wanted to be a history major. I accepted his offer and attended two or three of his seminars during that semester. But when the semester was over and I had my A from the good professor—and he was an excellent one—I was out of there and back on my entomology track.

YOU CAN'T SPOIL YOUR KIDS WITH AFFECTION

I have so many events in my growing up with my marvelous mother and father as well as utterly loving aunts and uncles that I hardly know which most memorable experience in this category to share with you at this time. "You cannot spoil your kids with affection" was all that I knew growing up between Topeka's Mud Town and the La Jolla Canyon, from Eads to Courier. Dad did not have many occasions to utter these words, but he parented them for me constantly at 807 Wood Street.

One lovely instance happened while he was very busily working on some construction project in our garage, which served as both our garage and his workshop. Dad turned out all kinds of wood worked marvels from yard figures to a glorious sled made just for me. I often stood in the doorway and watched him producing these magical works of creative art. On this very hot day, I was not standing there and watching him work his spell upon the wood; instead, I remember running into Dad's shop's side of the garage, crying about some major four-year-old's issue. As I recall the event, there was a lot of noise in the shop, and sawdust was flying all over the shop. Dad worked in the center of a great cloud of it; and a good friend of his, Vernon Fox,[1] and his brother John[2] were either helping Dad or watching him work— I am not sure which—but in any event, when I came bursting into that den of dust and noise, John Fox said to me that they were busy, blocking my path to Dad. He shouted to me to come back when they had finished their work. Dad looked at him with eyes that told him to shut up and quickly shut off the saw, motioning for me to come to him, which I did. The shop was suddenly very quiet. Dad listened to me

---

[1] Vernon Fox was Dad's barber too. He came to our house and cut Dad's hair regularly. Jellyroll, as he was always called, charged $25 for his very fast work, for which he was famous in Topeka. Well, Jellyroll gave me my first haircut. And one of my three-inch long braids was pressed in our big family Bible. That little braid, along with a lot of family memorabilia, is now a part of the John Fouts Gardenhire Family Collection at the University of Kansas's Spencer Research Library in Lawrence, Kansas.

[2] John Fox was the father of Marsha Jane Fox Davis, my lifelong friend whom I can remember from before we started kindergarten together at Washington Elementary School there in Mud Town. We have kept in touch for over fifty years now.

spill out my sad story at the end of which he put his great big hand on my back and pressed me to his side. I have, of course, forgotten what he said to me, but I felt totally comforted and was about to run off to other four-year-old concerns when Mr. Fox admonished Dad that he was spoiling me by letting me break into their adult activities. Dad told the two of them, "When you tell your kids that they can come to you anytime, you had better mean it, and I do. Besides, you cannot spoil your kids with affection." He laughed loudly as the noise of the workshop ensued. The expression on the faces of his two friends indicated that they did not know what he was talking about.

To this day, I can feel the affection and warmth and comfort of that moment when I was pressed against Dad's dust-covered side.

NEVER GET UPSET
OVER NOTHING

Quite upset, Mother returned from her Ladies' Conference Day committee planning session with the news that someone had "pinched" her new hat. It was a brown Dobbs pillbox felt number[1] that she was particularly fond of, having just gotten it to be featured as her "dress up" winter hat. OK, OK, but these were important to Mud Town ladies. Of course, Dad tried to inject the idea that her hat might be lost and not stolen, especially in that "holy circle of ladies." He did get that idea across, and it was not being well received. Mother was not amused and was prepared to rant on a bit more about the "theft of her lovely hat" when the phone rang. It was her good friend Mrs. Edna Burnette,[2] reporting that she had moved Mother's hat from the bed where the other coats and hats of the committee members were being piled up. She did so to keep Mother's new hat from being crushed out of shape by the growing number of garments that was being added to the pile as committee members continued to arrive and unwrap. Edna had been protecting Mother's hat by moving the hat from the bed and was upset that Mother had left the meeting before she had an opportunity to tell her the whereabouts of her vaunted hat. Edna had placed the hat on the bedroom dresser in full view, but Mother had not seen it sitting on the dresser because she did not expect to see it there. Well, arrangements were made to retrieve the hat that evening as soon as Mr. Burnette returned home from work and could deliver it to 807. The crisis over, Dad softly said to Mother as he rose from the dining room table, "You see, old lady, get upset after you know what the facts really

---

[1] This Dobbs hat was the same one that Mother wore in the rain sometime later. When she got home, water was standing in the brim of that wonderful hat. The hat was placed in the oven for some reason, and the following morning, the water was still standing in the brim of that hat. That fact spoke of the quality of the felt in the hat. I doubt that the Dobbs Company even knew of the fine quality of that hat. She and Dad often spoke of how great that hat was, especially when they were discussing some serious purchase that lay in the offing. "Always buy the best" meant something to the two of them.

[2] Mrs. Edna Burnette was the same friend of Mother's who was laughing so hard with her as they enumerated Dad's many admirable qualities. These two ladies remained close friends throughout their lives there in Mud Town.

are. Don't get upset over nothing." When he bent over and kissed her, she just beamed.

Another example of this saying occurred at a theater in Seattle many years ago, but the memory and impression of that event remain highly vivid for me. I was ushered down the aisle to my seat in Wheeler Hall on the University of Washington's campus. When I stepped in front of the early arrivals, one man did not get up or make any effort to let me pass. Immediately, I thought that I was being confronted by some "racist nutcase." Well, before I had puffed up to my most sharp-tongued state of being verbally defensive and upset, I realized that the man had no lower legs, which made standing a problem for him. OK, OK, I felt like a fool. I am glad to this day that I took a second look before I spoke to that poor fellow. So "don't get upset over nothing."

ADDENDUM

Dad had a number of other sayings that we all learned much from, growing up there in beautiful downtown Topeka.

- Be sure to put the top back on the can of paint while y.ou are painting.
- Don't look for trouble. It can find you without your help.
- Private thoughts should be just that—private!
- Don't tell everything that you know in one sitting.
- Do what you want to do, but do it without hurting anyone.
  He was an existentialist before his time. Well, maybe not; he could have read about that philosophy as it developed out of the Second World War in France, and he probably did, now that I think about it. He believed in limiting one's behavior to one's reach; therefore, one needed to be very responsible for oneself.
- When criticized, look for the truth in it. In every unjust criticism lies a disguised compliment.

These sayings followed almost any carping by us regarding something that some friend or foe said:

- You hear best when you listen to what is being said to you.
- Take only what you need and never more than you need.
  Dad would also present this saying in the form of a question. "Did you weigh the question?" Of course, this one asked us if we had thought about the question that we were being asked before we responded to it.

This saying was one that Dad often said to my sister, Ruth:

- You can't get a shirt off the back of a naked man.

Advice included:

- The only day that you are promised is the one that you are in, so make it joyful.

- Laugh out loud every day because happiness is like self-rising flour.
- Never adjust your cap while standing under your neighbor's pear tree.
- Never let a fool steal your joy. (After quoting this one to us, Dad would recite Countee Cullen's poem called "Incident.")
- Live with your spouse as if you two have just met.
- Avoid waiting for someone to make you happy because that train has left the station.
- The world is a banquet, so eat and never listen to anybody who tells you to fast in the face of it.
- Life is to be lived, not understood, so don't be an observer of it.
- Lead or follow. It's your choice.
- Watch out for things that are too good to be true. They probably are!
- Most *free things* are worth what you paid for them.
- You have a right to your own opinions.
- There is a difference between chicken salad and chicken shit.[1]
- Know the difference!

What wonderful information these words of life gave to a kid growing up in beautiful Topeka's Mud Town. And I now find that the older I get, the smarter Dad gets. The child is indeed the father of the man.

---

[1] This is the only four-letter word that I can remember Dad ever using, and it was never used in the presence of my mother. Around her, he preferred clusters of alliterative words to express annoyance, anger, or outrage. A few of his more choice examples include "totally, unredeemed, obdurate lout"; "a completely feckless, nugatory twit"; "freshly peeled, popping pustule of a person"; "a hissing horse's hind quarter"; or a "pigheaded, prurient, pee-stained cod purse," which he reserved for one Mr. Ben Bailey whom he detested mainly because the said gentleman was so publicly disrespectful of his wife.

Printed in the United States
100315LV00005B/524/A